Wild Game

C O O K B O O K

by Carol Ann Shipman

hancock

house

ISBN 0-88839-511-6
ISBN 0-88839-586-8 (Alaskan edition)
Copyright © 2004 Carol Ann Shipman

Cataloging in Publication Data
Shipman, Carol Ann, 1944–
    Wild game cookbook / Carol Ann Shipman.

    (Nature's gourmet series)
    Includes index.
    ISBN 0-88839-511-6 — ISBN 0-88839-586-8 (Alaskan ed.)

    1. Cookery (Game) I. Title. II. Series.
TX751.S54 2004   641.6'91   C2003-910996-8

All rights reserved. No part of this publication may be reproduced, stored
in a retrieval system or transmitted, in any form or by any means, elec-
tronic, mechanical, photocopying, recording, or otherwise, without the
prior written permission of Hancock House Publishers.
Printed in China—JADE

Editing: Nancy Miller
Series design and production: Nando DeGirolamo
Photographic sources listed on page 93

Published simultaneously in Canada and the United States by

HANCOCK HOUSE PUBLISHERS LTD.
19313 Zero Avenue, Surrey, B.C. V3S 9R9
(604) 538-1114 Fax (604) 538-2262

HANCOCK HOUSE PUBLISHERS
1431 Harrison Avenue, Blaine, WA 98230-5005
(604) 538-1114 Fax (604) 538-2262
Web Site: www.hancockhouse.com *email:* sales@hancockhouse.com

dedication

This book is dedicated to Nando's beautiful little girl Cassandra with love.

acknowledgments

I was very fortunate to work with a wonderful team to produce this book. I appreciate and thank all the people who were involved, and give special thanks to my daughter Kathryn Chan, for the long hours of editing the first draft, also my son-in-law David for the constant support and understanding testing endless recipes for all of the series. This one is for you!

To my publisher David Hancock, who shared my vision for the series, thank you for your patience and enthusiasm for this book.

Thanks again to Nando DeGirolamo, for his outstanding design for the entire series, that makes this book on first printing a best seller.

To my husband Richard Shipman, the bow hunter in the family, thank you for the long hours of hunting, making it possible to develop even more recipes for my Wild Game Cookbook.

A special thank you to Richard Groenheyde, production coordinator, for his talent to meet deadlines, and fine-tune the changes before printing.

Thank you.

Indoor Roses

Care Instructions

Please unpack and check your plant immediately on receipt,
adding water if necessary.

Position

Stand the rose indoors in a bright position, such as on a windowsill.
A temperature of between 13 and 21°C (55-70°F) is ideal.

Care

The compost should never be allowed to dry out completely, but equally
do not allow the plant to become waterlogged. Where possible, water
over a sink and allow any excess water to drain out. Adding some plant
food to the water every 10 days or so will help prolong flowering.

Remove any dying or damaged flowers or leaves as you see them.

Pot roses are designed to provide an indoor flower display of between 2
and 4 weeks. After flowering they can either be discarded, or you can try
planting outside in a patio container in late spring or summer, standing the
rose in a sunny but sheltered position. (Pot roses are grown in a heated
greenhouse, so sudden exposure to cold weather may kill the plant.)

Caution

Protect all surfaces as scratching or staining may occur.

IF YOU HAVE ANY QUESTIONS OR COMMENTS
PLEASE CALL 0333 014 8000

www.marksandspencer.com/flowers

contents

soup & salad

Always use tongs to turn game pieces over during cooking. This prevents the skin from being pierced, keeping the natural juices sealed inside the skin. Cut the meat and vegetables into uniform sizes and shapes to ensure even cooking. Keep the food in constant motion, tossing and stirring it with a flat metal or wooden spatula. This prevents it from burning and also seals in the flavor.

Game Bird Soup

SERVES 8 – 10		
1	**duck or pheasant**	1
	flour	
	salt and pepper to taste	
1/4 cup	**butter**	60 mL
2	**small onions**	2
1	**clove garlic** crushed	1
2	**carrots** diced	2
1/2 cup	**celery** diced	125 mL
8 cups	**canned chicken broth with rice**	2000 mL
2 cups	**burgundy wine**	500 mL
2-1/2 cups	**canned button mushrooms**	625 mL
2 tbsp	**minced parsley**	30 mL
	pinch of marjoram, thyme and basil	

Disjoint the duck or pheasant; roll the pieces in flour seasoned with salt and pepper. In large heavy fry pan sauté the game bird pieces alone with butter and onions cut into 1-inch pieces. Add crushed garlic, diced carrots and celery and sauté until lightly browned. Transfer mixture to a large soup pot. Stir in chicken broth with rice (canned variety will work fine). Add burgundy wine and drained mushrooms. Add spices and bring to a boil slowly, then simmer until the duck or pheasant is tender.

Goose Oyster Gumbo

SERVES 16 – 18		
5 lbs	**goose parts** legs, backs, wings, giblets	2270 g
1/2 cup	**vegetable oil**	125 mL
1/2 cup	**flour**	125 mL
2 cups	**onion** chopped	500 mL
1 cup	**bell pepper** chopped	250 mL
1/2 cup	**celery** chopped	125 mL
	salt, black pepper, hot sauce to taste	
12 cups	**hot water**	3000 mL
2 cups	**fresh oysters**	500 mL
1/2 cup	**green onion tops** chopped	125 mL
1/4 cup	**parsley** chopped	60 mL
	cooked rice	

Parboil goose parts in water to cover until meat is tender and falling from the bone. Remove from water, cool, and debone. Make a roux by cooking oil and flour in a large black-iron pot. Cook slowly over low heat until dark brown, stirring constantly. Add chopped onion, bell pepper and celery and cook until tender. Add salt, black pepper and hot sauce, then stir in hot water and goose meat. Cook over low heat in a covered pot for 1 hour. Stir in oysters, onion tops and parsley. Heat for 10 minutes and serve over rice.

L' Auberge Provençale Grilled Quail Salad

Marinate the quail in 1/4 cup (60 mL) of the vinaigrette for approximately 20 minutes. Remove them from marinade then grill quail on high heat approximately 4 minutes until they are medium-rare.

Place all vinaigrette ingredients in a bowl except the olive oil. Mix well with a whisk. While continuing to whisk the ingredients, gradually add the olive oil until it is incorporated. Set aside.

Salad

Arrange the salad greens on warm plates. Cut the quail in quarters. One whole quail for each salad. Arrange on plate. Make sure vinaigrette is well mixed and spoon over each salad.

SERVES 4 – 6

4-6	**quail**	4-6

VINAIGRETTE

1 cup	**white balsamic vinegar**	250 mL
2 tbsp	**shallots** chopped	30 mL
1 tbsp	**garlic** chopped	15 mL
2 tbsp	**fresh herbs** chopped (sage, rosemary, thyme)	30 mL
	salt and pepper to taste	
2 cups	**extra virgin olive oil**	500 mL
1 lb	**mixed field salad greens** washed and dried	454 g

Mexican Meat-Ball Soup

Sauté the onion and garlic in salad oil and add the tomato sauce and consommé. Mix the ground venison and pork and add the rice, salt, pepper and slightly beaten egg. Mix together and shape into small balls. Set aside. Bring the soup to a boil and drop in the meatballs. Cover and cook half an hour. In the last 10 minutes add the chili powder and the sprigs of mint leaves or dried mint.

SERVES 8

1	**onion** minced	1
1	**garlic clove** crushed	1
2 tbsp	**salad oil**	30 mL
1 cup	**tomato sauce**	250 mL
1/2 lb	**ground pork**	227 g
8 cups	**well-seasoned consommé or water with bouillon** powder or cubes	2000 mL
1/2 lb	**ground venison**	227 g
1/4 cup	**rice**	60 mL
1/2 tsp	**salt**	2 mL
1/4 tsp	**pepper**	1 mL
1	**egg**	1
1/2 tsp	**chili powder**	2 mL
	sprigs of mint leaves or pinch dried mint	

The Blom House Papa Jack's Duck and Shrimp Salad

SERVES 1

1	**duck breast**	1
4	**jumbo shrimp**	4
1 cup	**spring mix lettuce**	250 mL
3	**slices Bermuda onion**	3
1/4 cup	**red wine vinegar**	60 mL
2	**cloves garlic** chopped	2
	black pepper to taste	

BRANDY MANGO SAUCE

2 tbsp	**olive oil**	30 mL
1/2 cup	**Chardonnay**	125 mL
	juice of 1/2 lemon	

Toss spring mix lettuce with red wine vinegar and black pepper. Place in center of plate forming a mound. Sauté duck breast in pan with 1 tablespoon (15 mL) olive oil until skin is golden brown. Finish cooking in a 350°F (175°C) oven for 10 minutes. Sauté shrimp in 1 tablespoon (15 mL) of olive oil and add garlic, wine and the juice of 1/2 lemon. Cook until reduced. Place shrimp around lettuce. Slice duck breast and place a couple of slices between each shrimp. Place onion slice on top of lettuce mound. Pour brandy mango sauce over shrimp and duck breast.

Cajun-Fried Quail

SERVES 4

2	**boneless quail**	2
1 cup	**buttermilk**	250 mL
2 cups	**flour**	500 mL
1 tbsp	**each garlic powder, chili powder, paprika**	15 mL
1 tsp	**each cayenne pepper, salt and black pepper**	5 mL
	oil for deep-frying peanut oil preferred	

Marinate quail in buttermilk 15 minutes in a glass container or plastic bag. In a small bowl thoroughly combine flour, garlic powder, chili powder, paprika, cayenne, salt and black pepper. Set aside.

Heat oil in a deep fryer or Dutch oven to 375°F (190°C) . Remove quail from buttermilk and place in flour mixture, turning to coat well. Fry in oil about 8 minutes. Remove and drain on paper towels. Cut in halves.

Chef Kevin Durkin and Chef Andreas Camacho Cajun-Fried Quail Caesar Salad

Prepare dressing, quail and bread sticks. In a large bowl, toss romaine with dressing until all leaves are coated. Divide among 4 plates and sprinkle each with Parmesan cheese. Top each salad with half a Cajun-Fried quail and 2 Jalapeño Bread Sticks. Salt and freshly ground black pepper, to taste. Add freshly grated Parmesan cheese.

Caesar Dressing

In a small bowl whisk together egg yolk, lime juice, vinegar, Worcestershire sauce, mustard, anchovy and garlic. Slowly whisk in olive oil until emulsified (Alternatively, combine all ingredients except oil in a blender and purée. While motor is running, slowly pour olive oil in a thin, steady stream). Season with salt, pepper and Parmesan. Set aside. Season with added Parmesan before serving.

SERVES 4

1/3 cup	**Caesar Dressing** recipe follows	1/3 cup
	Cajun-Fried Quail (recipe page 10)	
	Jalapeño Bread Sticks (recipe page 21)	
2 tbsp	**Parmesan cheese** freshly grated or to taste	30 mL

CAESAR DRESSING

1	**egg yolk**	1
1 tbsp	**fresh lime juice**	15 mL
2 tbsp	**white wine vinegar**	30 mL
	dash of Worcestershire sauce	
1 tbsp	**Dijon mustard**	15 mL
2 tbsp	**anchovy paste** or mashed anchovies	30 mL
1-3/4 tsp	**garlic** chopped	7 mL
1 cup	**virgin olive oil**	250 mL
1 tbsp	**Parmesan cheese** freshly grated	15 mL

Chef Kevin Durkin and Chef Andreas Camacho Cajun-Fried Quail Caesar Salad

lunch

Forest mushrooms and juniper berries are compatible with all game meats. Always use seasoned butters to flavor game. Good side-dish choices for game include wild rice, pasta, rosemary potatoes and seasonal vegetables. Game, which is generally low in fat and high in protein, has become so popular that much is being farm-raised to meet increased demand, especially in restaurants.

Three-Alarm Buffalo Chili

SERVES 8

5 lbs	**buffalo stew meat** 3/4-inch cubes	2270 g
	oil for frying	
1-2	**jalapeño chilies** fresh or pickled	1-2
1	**large onion** chopped	1
4	**cloves garlic** minced or pressed	4
4 cups	**tomato sauce**	1000 mL
2 cups	**canned tomatoes**	500 mL
12 oz	**beer**	360 mL
2 tsp	**dried oregano**	10 mL
2 tsp	**black pepper** coarsely ground	10 mL
1-1/2 tbsp	**ground cumin**	22.5 mL
1 tbsp	**paprika**	15 mL
1/3 cup	**ground Pasilla chili or New Mexico chili**	75 mL

To prepare fresh jalapeños hold each by the stem over a gas flame or almost touching an electric burner on high, turning until chili is charred on all sides. Let chilies stand until cool. Wearing gloves (important: do not touch hands to eyes) pull blistered skin from chilies. Cut chilies finely; discard remainder. For pickled chilies cut off and discard stems and chop finely.

Add oil to pan over medium-high heat. Add meat, a portion at a time, and cook until well browned on all sides. Add onion, garlic and stir often until onion is limp, about 5 minutes. Stir in tomatoes, tomato sauce, chopped jalapeños, beer, oregano, pepper, cumin, paprika and ground Pasilla chili; stir well.

Bring to a boil, reduce heat, and simmer until meat is very tender, about 2 hours; stir occasionally. If chili is thinner than you like, uncover and simmer until some of the liquid evaporates. If it's thicker than you like, stir in water and bring to a boil. Add salt to taste.

Three-Alarm Buffalo Chili

Chef Todd Rogers Wild Venison Chili

Grind venison with bacon, then place in a Dutch oven over medium heat. Cook until no longer pink, then drain fat. Add onion, bell peppers, garlic, tomatoes, Chipotles, Anaheims, jalapeños, red pepper flakes, cumin, chili powder, salt, black pepper, tomato paste and 4 cups (1000 mL) stock. Simmer 1 hour. Meanwhile, remove and discard stems from cilantro and rosemary; chop leaves. Stir chopped cilantro and rosemary into chili, along with cherries, mushrooms, vinegar and bourbon. Simmer 30 minutes. Add remaining 2 cups (500 mL) stock, and simmer 20 minutes, or until thick. Adjust seasoning to taste. Serve with tortilla strips; sprinkle goat cheese atop each serving.

SERVES 15

5 lbs	**venison or other wild game meat**	2270 g
1 lb	**apple-smoked bacon**	454 g
1-1/2	**large or 2 medium sized sweet onions** diced	1-1/2
1	**each red, yellow and green bell peppers** seeded and diced	1
1	**large garlic clove** minced	1
3	**large tomatoes** seeded and cut into large cubes	3
3	**Chipotle peppers** (dried, smoked jalapeños) rehydrated	3
2	**dried Anaheim chilies** rehydrated	2
2	**jalapeños**	2
1 tbsp	**crushed red pepper flakes**	15 mL
1/4 cup	**ground cumin**	60 mL
1/2 cup	**chili powder**	125 mL
2 tbsp	**salt and freshly ground black pepper**	30 mL
1/4 cup	**tomato paste**	60 mL
6 cups	**game or chicken stock** divided	1500 mL
1/2	**bunch cilantro**	1/2
3	**sprigs rosemary**	3
1 cup	**sun-dried cherries**	250 mL
3 cups	**Shiitake mushrooms**	750 mL
3 tbsp	**balsamic vinegar** dark, aged Italian vinegar	45 mL
3 oz	**bourbon**	90 mL
6	**corn tortillas** julienned and fried crisp	6
3 oz	**goat cheese**	90 mL

Roland's Place Venison Pie with Medallions of Venison and Spaghetti Squash

SERVES 8

PIE DOUGH

3-1/2 cups	**flour**	875 mL
1/2 cup	**water**	125 mL
1 cup	**butter**	250 mL
1 tsp	**salt**	5 mL

VENISON MIX

1-1/2 lbs	**ground venison**	681 g
1	**carrot**	1
1	**leek**	1
2	**shallots**	2
1/2	**stalk celery**	1/2
1 cup	**shiitake mushrooms**	250 mL
1/4 cup	**tomato paste**	60 mL
	Cognac	
	Juniper berry, thyme, salt and pepper to taste	
1/4 cup	**red currant jelly**	60 mL
1 cup	**burgundy wine**	250 mL
	flour	

RED CURRANT SAUCE

	Venison stock	
	Shallots	
	Red wine	
1/2 cup	**currants**	125 mL
	Cognac	

SPAGHETTI SQUASH

	Spaghetti squash	
	Butter	
	Salt	
6	**2-ounce medallion venison**	6

Pie Dough
Mix all ingredients. Let rest 20 minutes. Roll 2/3 dough in individual mold. Reserve.

Venison Mix
Dice finely all vegetables; brown on stove. Add ground meat. Let cook 20 minutes. Add tomato paste and 2 tablespoons (30 mL) flour. Brown some more, flour and red currant jelly. Brown some more, flame with cognac. Add seasoning and wine. Cook slowly for 1 hour. Check seasoning and consistency. Let cool 1 hour. Cook slowly for 1 hour on low oven, about 200°F (95°C). Just keep an eye on it, some ovens have hot spots. The pastry should be golden brown.

Red Currant Sauce
Reduce wine and shallots; flame with cognac. Add stock and currants and adjust thickness.

Spaghetti Squash
Bake in oven for 1 hour; take meat out of shell and reserve.

Finish Pie
Place venison mix in pie mold. Cover with dough. Bake 30 minutes at 375°F (190°C) oven.

Finish Dish
Sear medallion in butter (keep medium-rare). Sauté spaghetti squash with butter. Place pie in middle of plate. Put medallion, then sauce, over pie. Place squash around venison.

Roland's Place Venison Pie with Medallions of Venison and Spaghetti Squash

Exotic Blues Burger

In a large bowl, mix 6 oz. (30 mL) House of Blues seasoning with ground exotic meat using 1 teaspoon (5 mL) per 8 oz. (250 mL) of meat.

Form ground meat into patties. Grill burgers, toast roll. Top with lettuce, tomato, onion and cheese.

SERVES 6

3 lbs	**ground exotic meat** kangaroo, buffalo, ostrich, venison, alligator, elk	1362 g
6	**brioche roll** or your favorite rolls	6
6 tsp	**House of Blues seasoning mix** recipe follows	30 mL
	lettuce	
	tomato slices	
	your favorite cheese	

HOUSE OF BLUES SEASONING MIX
Mix together and set aside until needed.

1/4 cup	**kosher salt**	60 mL
1 tbsp	**minced garlic**	15 mL
1 tbsp	**minced onion** and 1 teaspoon (5 mL)	15 mL
1 tbsp	**basil**	15 mL
1 tbsp	**thyme**	15 mL
1 tbsp	**oregano**	15 mL
1 tbsp	**black pepper**	15 mL

Venison Chili

SERVES 10 – 12

8-10 lbs	**venison**	3632 g
	or an inexpensive cut of beef	
2	**cloves elephant garlic**	2
1/2 cup	**water**	125 mL
12	**fresh red peppers**	12
6	**fresh jalapeño peppers**	6
	more if you like your chili hot	
3	**dried cayenne peppers**	3
1	**Habanero pepper**	1
	large fresh	
5	**white onions**	5
	large	
2-3	**Roma plum tomatoes**	2-3
3 tbsp	**dark chili powder**	45 mL
2 tbsp	**cumin**	30 mL
1 tbsp	**black pepper**	15 mL
	coarsely ground	
1-1/2 cups	**yellow cornmeal**	375 mL
2 cups	**potatoes**	375 mL
	chunked (optional)	

Trim fat from venison or beef. Set fat aside. Cut venison or beef into 1-inch cubes, sauté meat in large heavy saucepan. Mince garlic and sauté with a few pieces of the fat cut from the meat, leave garlic and the drippings in the pan and discard any solid fat. Brown the beef or venison cubes. Combine the water, meat, garlic and the drippings from the fry pan into a large covered pot on low heat. Peel and dice onions and potatoes, add to the pot. Seed and mince all peppers. Purée or mash tomatoes, add to the pot. Add cumin, black pepper, chili powder. Simmer for 2 hours loosely covered then add cornmeal. Allow this mixture to simmer (still covered) at least another 4–5 hours more. Add chili powder or cumin to taste.

Newberry Beefalo Farm Chili Rojo Concarne

SERVES 4 – 6

1 lb	**ground beefalo**	454 g
2 tbsp	**canola oil**	30 mL
4 tbsp	**chili powder**	60 mL
3/4 cup	**onion**	175 mL
	chopped	
1/2 tbsp	**garlic**	7.5 mL
1-1/2 cups	**diced tomatoes**	375 mL
1 tbsp	**vinegar**	15 mL
1 tsp	**ground coriander**	5 mL
1/8 tsp	**ground cloves**	0.5 mL
1 tsp	**cumin**	5 mL
2 tsp	**oregano**	10 mL
2 tsp	**brown sugar**	10 mL
3 cups	**beef consommé**	750 mL
1-1/2 cups	**red kidney beans**	375 mL
	drained	
1-1/2 cups	**pinto beans**	375 mL
	drained	

Brown beefalo in canola oil in a deep pan. Add onions and cook until tender. Combine all ingredients in pan and simmer for two hours.

Polish Pheasant Sandwich

Spread Polish mustard on bread. Place pheasant on bread. Place the cheese on top of the pheasant slices and put in microwave for 30 seconds. This recipe can also be grilled under the broiler.

SERVES 1

4	**large pieces of pheasant** cooked	4
2	**pieces of fresh bread**	2
1 tbsp	**Polish mustard**	15 mL
1	**slice of American cheese**	1

Venison Chili

Elk Katcha Korma

Elk Katcha Korma

Cube meat into 1-inch pieces. Sauté elk meat in oil. Add all the ingredients in order. Mix thoroughly. Simmer for 2 hours on low heat until meat is slightly tender. Place in casserole dish, cover with lid or foil. Cook in slow oven, 175°F (80°C) for about one hour longer until meat is very tender.

SERVES 6

4 lbs	**elk, deer, or antelope**	1816 g
1/3 cup	**cooking oil** or olive oil	75 mL
2 tsp	**salt**	10 mL
2 tbsp	**ginger** minced	30 mL
1 cup	**onions** minced	250 mL
1/3 cup	**yogurt**	75 mL
3 tsp	**ground coriander**	15 mL
1-2	**bay leaves**	1-2
1 tsp	**peppercorns**	5 mL
5	**whole cloves**	5
1/4 tsp	**peppercorns**	1 mL
2	**whole cardamoms**	2
1 cup	**water**	250 mL
2 tbsp	**beef browning or 1 cube of beef bouillon**	30 mL

Jalapeño Bread Sticks

Thaw puff pastry if frozen. Roll out 1/8-inch thickness and cut into 10 x 1-inch strips. Brush with egg water mixture, then sprinkle with Parmesan cheese and jalapeños. Twist each strip 4-6 times to produce a spiral. Line a cookie sheet with parchment paper (necessary to keep from sticking), and then place strips on parchment. Bake in 350°F (175°C) oven 15 minutes, or until lightly golden. Let cool before serving.

SERVES 4

4 oz.	**puff pastry** can use frozen	113.4 g
1	**egg** blended with 2 tablespoon (30 mL) water	1
1 oz	**Parmesan cheese** fresh grated	28 g
1 oz	**jalapeños** finely chopped pickled, seeded	28 g

Steve Amaral's BBQ Ulupalukua Venison with Summer Vegetables

Clean the tenderloin. Add the olive oil, herbs, salt and pepper and let set for a few hours before broiling. Cook tenderloin until medium-rare. Blanch the carrots and yellow and green beans in boiling water for 1 minute. Shock in ice cold water. Let dry and set aside. Mix the carrots, yellow and green beans, Italian parsley, tomatoes in olive oil and salt and pepper to taste. Mix demi glaze and mushroom juice together and bring to a boil. Slice cooked meat in 1/4-inch thick slices. Lay 3 to 4 slices over the vegetables. Pour the sauce around the meat and garnish with mushroom caps and basil sprig. Drizzle basil oil over vegetables.

SERVES 2

6 oz	**venison tenderloin**	170 g
4 tbsp	**olive oil**	60 mL
1/4 cup	**herbs** chopped fresh	60 mL
2 tbsp	**carrots**	30 mL
2 tbsp	**beans** yellow	30 mL
2 tbsp	**beans** green	30 mL
1 tbsp	**tomato** julienne	15 mL
1 tsp	**Italian parsley** chopped	5 mL
4	**shiitake mushroom**	4
1/2 cup	**demi glaze**	125 mL
4 tbsp	**mushroom juice**	60 mL
2 tbsp	**basil oil**	30 mL
2	**sprigs basil**	2

Pizza with Duck Sausage

SERVES 4

DUCK SAUSAGE

2	**ducks**	2
	deboned, cubed or thickly sliced	
1 cup	**lean pork**	250 mL
1 cup	**lean beef**	250 mL
1	**shallot**	1
	minced	
1 tsp	**rosemary**	5 mL
2 tbsp	**Cognac**	30 mL
3/4 cup	**dry white wine**	175 mL
salt and white pepper to taste		
1	**Italian bread pizza round**	1
1/2	**red bell pepper**	1/2
	grilled then diced or thinly slivered	
2 tbsp	**olive oil**	30 mL
2 tbsp	**chili oil**	30 mL
3	**garlic cloves**	3
	minced and added to oil	

TOPPING

1 cup	**Mozzarella cheese**	250 mL
	grated	
1 cup	**Fontina cheese**	250 mL
sprinkle of fresh oregano and thyme		
onion slices		
mushrooms		
(optional)		

Combine duck, pork and beef. Cook over medium heat in heavy skillet, add rosemary, Cognac, dry white wine, salt and pepper. Cook until desired doneness. Use another small skillet and sauté garlic and shallots; add red pepper, olive oil, and chili oil. Spread oil and peppers on pizza round, then layer meat and sprinkle with cheeses, onion slices, mushrooms and spices. The pizza round is ready made and the meat is cooked so you are only melting the cheese. Bake at 350°F (175°C) until cheese is melted. Serve.

Alternative

Use your favorite pizza dough, following package instructions, or a frozen pizza crust in place of Italian bread pizza round.

Pizza with Duck Sausage

Venison Chili with Chorizo and Beer

Cut venison into 1/2-inch cubes. Toss with Ancho chili powder, cover and marinate 2 to 3 hours at room temperature. Remove casings from Chorizo sausage. Crumble and brown Chorizo in a large braising pan. Add venison and onions; cook, stirring until venison is browned and onions are translucent. Mix in flour, cook, stirring constantly, about 3 minutes. Add remaining ingredients and bring to a boil. Reduce heat and simmer, stirring occasionally for 2 to 3 hours until venison is tender and the sauce is thick.

SERVES 10

5 lbs	**venison leg or shoulder roast**	2270 g
1/2 cup	**Ancho chili powder**	125 mL
2-1/2 lbs	**Chorizo sausages**	1135 g
4 cups	**onion** chopped	1000 mL
1-1/2 cups	**masa flour**	375 mL
7-1/2 cups	**beer**	1875 mL
12 cups	**canned tomatoes with liquid**	3000 mL
4 cups	**chicken stock**	1000 mL
1/2 cup	**chopped garlic**	125 mL
1/4 cup	**dried oregano**	60 mL
3 tbsp	**ground cumin**	45 mL
1-1/2 tbsp	**salt**	22.5 mL
1 tbsp	**pepper**	15 mL

Sautéed Dijon Burgers

Mix ground meat, Dijon mustard, onion, egg, vinegar, pepper, celery flakes and bread crumbs. Form into patties, about 1-inch thick.

Heat oil in sauté pan and cook burgers over medium heat for about 4 minutes per side, until just cooked through. Serve on buns with tomato, lettuce and condiments; or serve on toasted sourdough bread with wine sauce.

SERVES 3

1 lb	**ground buffalo, kangaroo, ostrich, or venison**	454 g
2 tbsp	**Dijon mustard**	30 mL
2 tbsp	**onion** fresh, minced	30 mL
1	**egg**	1
3 tsp	**balsamic vinegar**	15 mL
1/4 tsp	**coarsely ground pepper**	1 mL
1 tbsp	**dried celery flakes**	15 mL
1/4 cup	**fine dry bread crumbs**	60 mL
1 tbsp	**olive oil**	15 mL

birds

People have gone wild over game in the past few years. Restaurant menus are dotted with quail, pheasant, venison, wild boar, elk, buffalo, goose and duck. Use berries (including huckleberries) and fresh herbs, such as lavender and sage leaves, rosemary and thyme as seasonings. Quail gets a flavor lift from gingered pears poached in port wine with fresh basil.

Grilled Grouse Sandwich

1-1/2 cups	**grilled or cooked grouse** cubed	375mL
6 tbsp	**oil** divided	90 mL
1 cup	**tomato paste**	250 mL
1 cup	**pimiento** chopped	250 mL
1-1/2 cups	**mushroom pieces** fresh or canned and drained	375 mL
1/8 tsp	**garlic powder**	0.5 mL
	French bread	
1 cup	**cheddar cheese** shredded	250 mL
1/4 cup	**green and red pepper slices** can use lesser amount of green pepper	60 mL

Sauté peppers, grouse, mushrooms in small amount of hot olive oil, set aside. Combine oil, tomato paste, garlic powder. Mix well. Cut French bread in half lengthwise. Spread cheese on both sides of the open face French bread, spread next with oil, tomato paste and garlic mixture, then pimientos. Place even amount of pepper, grouse, mushroom mixture on each side of the bread. Sprinkle with small amount of cheese. Place under broiler until cheese mixture melts.

Topping
Sprinkle of cheese of your choice.

Grilled Grouse Sandwich

L' Auberge Provencale Chesapeake B & B Liqueur Game Hen

Preheat oven to 350°F (175°C) degrees. In large skillet over medium heat, heat 1 tablespoon (15 mL) olive oil until very hot. Add celery and onion and cook until tender-crisp. Remove from heat and stir in crabmeat and bread crumbs.

Season cavity of each hen with salt, pepper and Old Bay Seasoning. Sprinkle each hen cavity with 1 teaspoon (5 mL) B & B liqueur. Divide crabmeat mixture into equal parts, stuff into each hen and truss for roasting. Lightly dust each hen with flour. In large ovenproof skillet over medium-high heat, heat remaining olive oil and butter. Place hens in skillet and brown lightly. Drain all but 2 tablespoons (30 mL) oil; add whole shallots and bake for 25 to 35 minutes until juices run clear when hens are pierced with a fork, keep warm while making sauce.

Sauce

Remove hens from skillet; reserve juices (skim any fat, discard). Increase heat to high; add B & B liqueur to the pan juices and reduce by 1/2. Add cream, reduce until slightly thickened. Add demi-glace. Place shallots in sauce and reheat, add salt and pepper to taste.

Serve by placing a hen on each of four heated plates; make a line of sauce on each side of hen, place shallot on each line.

SERVES 4

4 tbsp	**olive oil**	60 mL
1	**celery stalk** minced	1
1	**medium-sized onion** minced	1
1-1/4 cups	**crabmeat** shell removed, flaked	310 mL
2 tbsp	**bread crumbs**	30 mL
4	**Cornish hens** deboned (about 1 pound each)	4
	salt and pepper to taste	
1 tbsp	**Old Bay Seasoning**	15 mL
4 tbsp	**B & B liqueur**	60 mL
2 tbsp	**butter**	30 mL
3 tbsp	**flour**	45 mL
2	**small shallots** minced	2

SAUCE

2 tbsp	**B & B liqueur**	30 mL
4 tbsp	**veal demi-glace**	60 mL
1 cup	**cream**	250 mL
	salt and pepper to taste	

Quail with Rosemary and Balsamic Vinegar Sauce

SERVES 4

8	**quail**	8
1/4 cup	**butter** divided	60 mL
3/4 cup	**beef broth**	175 mL
1/2 cup	**balsamic vinegar**	125 mL
1 tbsp	**fresh rosemary leaves** or 1 teaspoon (5 mL) dried	15 mL
rosemary springs for garnish		

Rinse quail and pat dry. Melt 2 tablespoons (30 mL) butter in a 10-inch frying pan over medium high heat. Add birds and brown lightly on all sides, about 10 minutes. Breast meat should be red and moist at the bone; to check, cut from just above the wing joint to breastbone. Lift birds into a serving dish to keep warm. To pan, add broth, vinegar, and rosemary. Over high heat, boil, uncovered until reduced to 1/2 cup (125 mL) about 5 minutes. Add remaining butter; stir constantly over medium heat until smoothly blended. Pour sauce over birds and garnish with rosemary.

Roasted Quail

SERVES 4

4	**quail** whole	4
6 tbsp	**butter** melted	90 mL
3 tbsp	**cognac**	45 mL
1-2 tsp	**lemon juice**	15-30 mL
30	**white grapes** cut in half and seeded	30
2	**apples** peeled cored and sliced	2
1/4 cup	**Vermouth**	60 mL
1 cup	**chicken broth**	250 mL
salt and pepper to taste		

Rinse quail under cool tap water, pat dry and place in shallow baking pan. Baste outside with butter and season lightly with salt and pepper. Place 1 tablespoon (15 mL) of butter in each cavity along with 1/2 slice of apple and a couple of grapes. Drizzle with cognac. Roast at 400°F (205°C) for 15 minutes basting every 5 minutes. Place the balance of the grapes around the outside of the birds and roast another 15 minutes. Remove quail and keep warm. Combine the remaining apples, Vermouth, chicken stock and pan juices and heat through. Stir well. Serve quail with sauce over top.

Barbecued Quail with Jalapeño Jelly Glaze

Remove necks and giblets; reserve for other uses. Cut through the backbone of each bird with poultry shears or a knife. Place quail, skin side up, on a flat surface and press firmly, cracking bones slightly, until bird lies flat. In a pan, combine butter and jelly. Stir over medium heat until melted. Stir in lime juice; set aside. Place quail, skin side up, on a lightly greased grill 4 to 6 inches above a solid bed of hot (not medium) coals. During cooking turn several times during the last 5 minutes, baste with jelly mixture. Cook quail until skin is browned and breast meat is cooked through, but still slightly pink near bone; cut to test (7 to 8 minutes). Sprinkle with salt and pepper before serving.

SERVES 6 –8

18-24	**quail**	18-24
1/4 cup	**butter or margarine**	60 mL
2/3 cup	**jalapeño jelly**	150 mL
2 tbsp	**lime juice**	30 mL
	salt and pepper	

Braised Quail in Juniper

Simmer beef consommé, chicken stock, Port wine, bay leaf and thyme for approximately 30 to 45 minutes or until 2 cups (500 mL) of stock remains. Strain and set aside. Dredge the quail in seasoned flour and brown in a large frying pan with the oil. Remove and set aside. Add the shallots, juniper berries to the pan and sauté until the shallots are tender return the quail to the pan along with the wine broth and cream. Simmer gently for 20 to 30 minutes, turning occasionally. Salt and pepper to taste.

SERVES 4

8	**quail**	8
2-1/2 cups	**beef consommé**	625 mL
2-1/2 cups	**chicken broth**	625 mL
2 cups	**Port wine**	500 mL
1	**bay leaf**	1
1	**sprig thyme**	1
3 tbsp	**olive oil**	45 mL
6	**banana shallots** large sliced, peeled and chopped	6
15	**juniper berries** crushed	15
1 cup	**whipping cream**	250 mL
1 cup	**seasoned flour**	250 mL
	salt and pepper to taste	

Lemon Butter Quail

SERVES 4

8	**quail**	8
1/2 cup	**butter**	125 mL
1/4 cup	**lemon juice**	60 mL
2 tbsp	**lemon peel** minced	30 mL
1/4 cup	**diced garlic**	60 mL
1/4 cup	**green onions** sliced	60 mL
8	**slices bacon**	8
1/4 cup	**parsley** chopped	60 mL
	salt and pepper to taste	
	Louisiana pepper sauce	
1 tsp	**cornstarch**	5 mL
1/2 cup	**warm water**	125 mL

Preheat oven to 350°F (175°C) degrees. In a large cast iron skillet melt butter over medium-high heat. Add lemon juice, peel, garlic and green onions. Sauté 3–5 minutes or until vegetables are wilted. Wrap bacon strip around each quail breast and hold in place with a toothpick. Place quail, breast side up in a 9- x 12-inch baking pan and drape with foil. Thoroughly baste each bird with butter sauce. Bake for 20 minutes, basting occasionally to prevent birds from drying out. After 20 minutes remove foil, turn birds breast side down and brown 10 additional minutes. Remove birds and keep warm. For gravy dissolve cornstarch in warm water and add to drippings in baking dish. Add Louisana pepper sauce. Stir over low heat, reduce to 1/2 volume and adjust seasonings if necessary. Return birds to baking dish and baste with gravy prior to serving. Garnish with parsley.

Lemon Butter Quail

Cliff House Chef Craig Hartman Maple Smoked Duck Breast with Sweet and Sour Salpicon of Apples

Combine maple syrup, kosher salt, black pepper, and marjoram and marinate breasts overnight. Sear duck breasts, skin side down, over medium heat until dark brown and most of the fat is rendered out. Using a home smoker, smoke breast flesh side down, over hickory wood for 20 minutes. Do not allow temperature to rise over 200°F (95°C) degrees. Cool and slice thin on the bias against the grain.

Salpicon of Apples

Combine all ingredients. Place 3 ounces (90 mL) of apple on plate and flatten to make a bed for the slices of duck. Sprinkle extra chopped parsley around edge of plate and serve.

Brunoise

Small Dice; 1/8-inch cube is the standard. For a brunoise cut, items are first cut in julienne, then cut crosswise. For a fine brunoise, 1/16-inch square, cut items first in fine julienne.

SERVES 4

1	**10–12 ounce duck breast** split and trimmed	1
1/2 cup	**pure maple syrup**	125 mL
1 tsp	**kosher salt**	5 mL
1/2 tsp	**cracked black pepper**	2 mL
1 tsp	**fresh marjoram** chopped	5 mL

SALPICON OF APPLES

2	**large apples** peeled, seeded and cut into small dice	2
2 tbsp	**each red, green and yellow bell pepper** cut brunoise	30 mL
1/4 cup	**raspberry vinegar**	60 mL
1/2 cup	**sugar**	125 mL
1/4 tsp	**salt**	1 mL
1 tsp	**fresh parsley** chopped	5 mL

Pheasant with Mustard Sauce

SERVES 4

2	**whole pheasants** deboned and cut in half	2
1/4 cup	**margarine**	60 mL
1 cup	**Shiitake mushrooms** sliced	250 mL
1/3 cup	**shallots** chopped	75 mL
1/3 cup	**dry white wine** such as Chardonnay	75 mL
2 tsp	**Dijon mustard**	10 mL
1 tsp	**country style Dijon mustard** with seeds	5 mL
1 cup	**pheasant or chicken broth**	250 mL
1/4 cup	**whipped cream**	60 mL
	salt and pepper to taste	

In medium-size skillet, melt margarine over medium heat. Add pheasant and sauté until light-golden brown. Remove from skillet and place in a shallow baking dish; bake in a 325°F (160°C) oven 5 to 10 minutes while you make the sauce. In same skillet in which pheasant was cooked, combine mushrooms and shallots and sauté 2 minutes. Add wine and let simmer 3 minutes to reduce. Add both styles of mustard and sauté 2 minutes. Add broth and let simmer 4 minutes to reduce. Stir in cream and adjust seasoning with salt and pepper.

Pheasant with Mustard Sauce

Chef Les Kincaid's Roast Duck Breast with Balsamic and Apricot

Sauce

In a heavy saucepan cook shallot in (5 mL) 1 teaspoon butter over moderately low heat, stirring, until softened. Carefully add both Port and brandy and boil until reduced by half. Add demi-glace and simmer for 5 minutes, or until reduced to about 2/3 cup. Pour sauce through a fine sieve into a small bowl and return to pan. Stir in apricot, vinegar, and salt and pepper to taste. Simmer sauce until apricot is just heated through and stir in remaining tablespoon (15 mL) butter.

Duck

Put duck breasts, skin sides down, on a cutting board. Using a sharp knife and following shape of breast trim all sinews, excess skin, and fat. With a fork carefully prick skin all over without piercing meat. Heat an ovenproof cast-iron skillet over moderately high heat until hot and add oil, swirling skillet until coated evenly. Pat duck dry and season with salt and pepper. Put duck, skin sides down, in skillet. Reduce heat to moderate and cook duck until skin is deep golden, about 3 minutes. Turn duck over and cook 2 minutes more. Remove duck from skillet and pour off fat. Return duck, skin sides down, to skillet and roast in meddle of oven 5 minutes for medium-rare. Keep duck warm and reheat sauce over low heat. Slice duck on the diagonal and serve with sauce.

SERVES 4 – 6

SAUCE		
1/4 cups	**shallots** minced	60 mL
1 tbsp	**cold sweet butter** plus 1 teaspoon (5 mL)	20 mL
1/2 cup	**Tawny Port**	125 mL
1 tbsp	**Brandy**	15 mL
1 cup	**duck-and-veal demi-glace** 6-1/2 ounce container stirred together with 3 tbsp (45 mL) water	
1/3 cup	**julienne strips dried apricot**	75 mL
1 tbsp	**balsamic vinegar**	15 mL
2	**1-pound boneless duck breasts with skin** (Long Island or Peking) halved	2
1 tsp	**canola oil**	5 mL

Chef Les Kincaid Grilled Duck Breast with Black Currants

SERVES 6

2 cups	**wine** Cabernet Sauvignon	500 mL
1/2 cup	**black currants** fresh or frozen	125 mL
2 tbsp	**cassis syrup**	30 mL
1/2 cup	**duck stock**	125 mL
6	**duck breasts** 6-8 ounces each	6
Kosher salt and freshly ground white pepper to taste		

Place the wine, half the black currants, and the cassis syrup in a medium-size saucepan and boil over moderate heat until the wine has reduced to about 1 cup (250 mL) 8 to 10 minutes. Add the stock and continue boiling until it has reduced by half, 5 to 7 minutes more. Strain out and discard the black currants, season the sauce to taste, and keep warm.

While the sauce is reducing, preheat the grill or broiler until very hot. Season the duck breasts with salt and pepper and cook them, with the skin side facing the heat, until crisp and brown, about 3 minutes; halfway through the cooking, rotate them 90 degrees to give them crosshatched grill marks. Then flip them and cook abut 3 minutes more, until medium-rare, still pink in the center. With a sharp knife, cut each breast at a 45-degree angle into slices about 1/4-inch thick. Arrange each breast on a heated serving plate. Spoon the sauce over it and scatter the remaining black currants on top.

Fried Quail with Sausage and Oyster Cream

Preheat the oven to its lowest setting and place a cooking rack over a sheet pan in the oven. Rinse the quail, pat dry, then dust in the flour. Do not season the flour; the sausage is very salty and spicy. Fry the quail in a small amount of oil or lard in a skillet over high heat until they are golden brown, turning once, about 10 minutes. Remove to the rack in the oven to keep them warm while you prepare the cream sauce. Drain the oysters and set aside, reserving the liquor. Put the sausages in a saucepan and cook over medium high heat until all of the grease is rendered out and the sausage is evenly browned. Remove the sausage from the pan and allow it to drain. Pour off the grease and discard. Add the cream and the oyster liquor to the pan and reduce over high heat until the sauce is just shy of the desired consistency, stirring often and scraping any brown bits stuck to the bottom of the pan. Lower the heat and crumble the cooked sausages into the cream. Add the oysters, heating the sauce through until the oysters just begin to curl, just a minute or two. Remove the birds from the oven to plates. Pour the sauce over the birds, dividing the oysters and bits of sausages equally among the plates.

SERVES 2 main course or 4 appetizers		
4	**quail** dressed for cooking	4
	flour for dusting	
	lard or oil for pan frying	
1 cup	**shucking oysters and their liquor**	250 mL
1/4 lb	**country sausages**	113.5 g
1 cup	**cream**	250 mL

Quail in Raspberry Sauce

SERVES 8

16	**quail**	16
3 tbsp	**salad oil**	45 mL

SAUCE

1/3 cup	**sugar**	75 mL
1/2 cup	**raspberry vinegar** or red wine vinegar divided	125 mL
2 cups	**chicken broth**	500 mL
1-1/2 tbsp	**cornstarch**	22.5 mL
1-1/2 tbsp	**water**	22.5 mL
1 cup	**unsweetened raspberries** fresh or partially thawed	250 mL
2 tbsp	**brandy**	30 mL
2 tbsp	**lemon juice**	30 mL
	salt and pepper to taste	

Rinse quail and pat dry; save necks and giblets for another use. Pour 2 tablespoons (30 mL) oil into a 10-inch skillet over medium high heat. Add birds a few at a time (do not crowd), and brown all over about 5 minutes per bird; add oil as needed. Arrange birds, breast up and slightly apart on a rack in a roasting pan. Roast birds in 400°F (205°C) oven until breasts are still red and moist in center but not wet-looking (cut into breast just above wing joint to test), 12 to 15 minutes. Remove birds to a platter; if needed, keep warm in low oven up to 30 minutes. Reserve roasting juices.

Sauce

To the frying pan add sugar and 1 tablespoon (15 mL) vinegar. Cook over medium high heat until sugar liquifies and turns a golden caramel color 3 to 5 minutes. While stirring add remaining vinegar; simmer, stirring until caramel dissolves about 2 minutes. Add broth and quail roasting juices; boil uncovered, until reduced by 1/2, about 15 minutes. Mix cornstarch and water stir in to sauce. Stir until boiling. Add raspberries, brandy. Lemon juice, salt and pepper to taste. Pour sauce over the birds and serve.

Hidden Creek Chef Rose Ludwig Roasted Breast of Duck with Raspberry Sauce and Wild Rice Pancakes

Sauté the garlic in the olive oil for one minute then add wine to the pan. Reduce the wine by half and then stir in the jam and chicken stock. Reduce this mixture by one-third; add the sage and pepper to taste. Set aside.

Lightly salt and pepper the duck and place skin side down in a skillet or sauté pan heated to a medium heat. cook slowly for 10 to 15 minutes until the skin is brown and some of the fat has been rendered out. If you do this step too quickly, the fat will not render out, but will be seared under the skin. Remove from the pan and roast on a rack in a roasting pan for 10 to 15 minutes until medium-rare. Remove from the oven, and allow the duck to rest for 5 minutes before slicing. Slice against the grain on an angle into about 4 or 5 pieces.

Wild Rice Pancakes

Mix all the ingredients together. Cook on either a lightly greased griddle or a large frying pan at medium-high heat. Once the pan is heated, using 1/4 cup (60 mL) of batter for each pancake, ladle batter onto the griddle so that the cakes are about 4 inches apart. When the edges are slightly browned and bubbles on the surface begin to pop, flip the cakes and continue cooking until they done all the way through. To serve, lay two of the pancakes on the edge of a dinner plate and arrange the duck slices on top of the sauce.

SERVES 4

4	**full duck breasts** split into halves	4
1 tbsp	**olive oil**	15 mL
2	**garlic cloves** minced	2
1/2 cup	**red wine** preferably Cabernet Sauvignon	125 mL
2 cups	**chicken stock**	500 mL
1/2 cup	**seedless raspberry jam**	125 mL
1 tsp	**finely chopped fresh sage**	5 mL
4 tbsp	**unsalted butter** room temperature	60 mL
	salt and pepper to taste	

WILD RICE PANCAKES

2	**eggs**	2
4 tbsp	**unsalted butter** melted	60 mL
1-1/4 cups	**flour**	310 mL
2 tsp	**sugar**	10 mL
4 tsp	**baking powder**	20 mL
1 tsp	**salt**	5 mL
1/2 tsp	**black pepper**	2 mL
2 cups	**milk**	500 mL
2 cups	**cooked wild rice**	500 mL

The Red Castle Inn Roasted Game Hens with Espresso Sauce

SERVES 4

4	**Cornish game hens**	4
	454 g (1 pound) each	
1 tsp	**salt**	5 mL
1/2 tsp	**fresh black pepper**	2 mL
2	**slices lemon**	2
	cut in half	

SAUCE

1/2 cup	**espresso**	125 mL
	or strong coffee	
2 tbsp	**brandy**	30 mL
2 tbsp	**fresh lemon juice**	30 mL
1/2 tsp	**Dijon mustard**	2 mL
1/4 tsp	**paprika**	1 mL
3 tbsp	**unsalted butter**	45 mL
	or margarine	
8	**medium shallots**	8
	peeled and left whole	

Combine sauce ingredients in a small saucepan. Heat to boiling, lower to simmer and cook one minute. Place oven rack in lower third of oven and preheat to 375°F (190°C) degrees. Rinse hens with cold water, dry well. Season cavities with salt and pepper. Place half slice lemon in each, divide 1 tablespoon (15 mL) espresso sauce equally between each cavity. Tie or skewer hens and roast breast side up in a shallow baking pan. Brush with a little sauce and cover loosely with a foil tend. Roast for 30 minutes, remove foil and brush with sauce. Roast 30 to 45 minutes longer until juices run clear when pricked. Cover again with tent if necessary to prevent over browning. Remove to heated platter and keep warm.

The Inn at New Berlin Chambord Roasting Duck

SERVES 4

4	**young duck**	4
	halves	
1 cup	**blackberry**	250 mL
	preserves	
2/3 cup	**sugar**	150 mL
3 tbsp	**cider vinegar**	45 mL
2/3 cup	**Chambord liqueur**	150 mL
1/2 cup	**chicken stock**	125 mL
1 tbsp	**flour**	15 mL
1 tbsp	**water**	15 mL

Mix 1 tablespoon (15 mL) flour to 1 tablespoon (15 mL) of water for each cup of sauce.

Preheat oven to 350°F (175°C) degrees. Combine all ingredients except duck in a heavy saucepan on medium heat until it reaches a boil. Simmer for 5 to 10 minutes on low heat, stirring constantly to avoid scorching. Coat each duck half with 2 tablespoons (30 mL) of sauce. Bake for 25 to 30 minutes or until skin is crispy. Thicken the remaining sauce with equal portions of a flour and water mixture until it coats the back of a spoon. Drizzle the remaining thickened sauce over cooked duck and serve on warm plate.

The Red Castle Inn Roasted
Game Hens with Espresso Sauce

main course

*Use natural seasonings that are compatible with the animal's diet —
berries, herbs, fruits and nuts. Dried cherries are particularly good with
venison in marinades and sauces. The most popular selection of wild
game on a menu today is currently a mixed grill of emu and venison
medallions, boneless quail breast and buffalo rib eye.*

Three Chimneys Inn Executive Chef Layne Thomas Grilled Ostrich Loin with Swedish Lingonberries

SERVES 4

4- 8 oz	**pieces ostrich loin**	4- 227 g
4	**bacon slices**	4
	salt and pepper to taste	
1/2 cup	**lingonberry jelly**	125 mL
1/2 cup	**chicken glaze**	125 mL
6 tbsp	**shallots** minced	90 mL
4	**rosemary sprigs**	4

Wrap one bacon slice around each ostrich loin, sandwiching in the rosemary sprig. Skewer with a wooden toothpick. Sprinkle with salt and pepper. Sear the loin in a hot skillet and place in a 375°F (190°C) oven. Cook to medium, no more. Brown the shallots in the searing pan and add the lingonberry jelly and chicken glaze. After removing the ostrich loin from the oven, remove the bacon and slice into very thin strips. Top with lingonberry glaze.

Herb Marinated Ostrich Steaks

SERVES 2

2-4	**small ostrich steaks**	2-4
1/4 cup	**light olive oil**	60 mL
2/3 cup	**balsamic vinegar**	150 mL
2 tbsp	**garlic** minced	30 mL
1 tbsp	**rosemary**	15 mL
1 tbsp	**thyme**	15 mL
1 tsp	**parsley flakes**	5 mL
1 tsp	**coarse black pepper**	5 mL

Combine all ingredients except meat in a glass baking dish. Place meat in dish and turn to coat, then pierce once or twice with a fork. Cover and place in refrigerator for about one hour, turning occasionally. Remove meat from marinade and place meat on rack in broiler pan 3–4 inches from heat. Broil 25 to 30 minutes for medium-rare to medium. Turn once during cooking. Also can be cooked on barbecue.

Simply the Best Ostrich Burgers

Combine all ingredients into a bowl and mix thoroughly. Form into desired size of patties and grill or fry to medium-well to well done.

SERVES 2

1-1/2 lbs	**ostrich meat** ground	681 g
1	**small onion** chopped fine	1
1/4 cup	**green pepper** chopped fine	60 mL
1	**package taco seasoning mix**	1
1/3 cup	**ketchup**	75 mL
1	**egg** beaten	1
1 tsp	**parsley flakes**	5 mL
1 tsp	**garlic salt**	5 mL

Simply the Best Ostrich Burgers

SERVES 2

2 lbs	**ostrich meat** ground	908 g
1/4 cup	**light cream**	60 mL
1/4 cup	**milk**	60 mL
2 tbsp	**onion** minced	30 mL
2 tbsp	**oil**	30 mL

MUSHROOM WINE SAUCE

2 tbsp	**butter**	30 mL
2 tbsp	**flour**	30 mL
1/4 cup	**flour**	60 mL
3/4 cup	**red wine**	175 mL
1 tbsp	**Worcestershire sauce**	15 mL
2 tbsp	**parsley flakes**	30 mL
10 oz	**can mushrooms** drained and rinsed	310 mL
2	**slices of buttered toast**	2

Ostrich Patties in Mushroom Wine Sauce

In a large bowl mix together meat, cream, milk and onion. Shape into patties. Heat oil in skillet and brown meat on both sides then remove and set aside. In the same skillet, melt butter, stir in flour, water and wine then thicken. Add Worcestershire sauce, parsley and mushrooms, then return patties to skillet. Cover and simmer 20 minutes basting occasionally. Place two patties on a slice of toast and spoon sauce over top before serving.

SERVES 5 – 6

2 lbs	**ground elk**	908 g
2 cups	**pinto or red beans**	500 mL
4 cups	**water** to cook beans	1000 mL
2	**medium garlic cloves** finely chopped	2
1	**large onion** chopped	1
1	**medium green bell pepper** chopped	1
2 tbsp	**flour**	30 mL
4 cups	**tomatoes** canned including liquid	1000 mL
2 cups	**tomato sauce**	500 mL
1 cup	**water**	250 mL
1/4 tsp	**salt**	1 mL
1/4 tsp	**pepper**	1 mL
2 tbsp	**ground cumin**	30 mL
2 tbsp	**unsweetened baking cocoa**	30 mL
2 tbsp	**chili powder** or to taste	30 mL

Cougar Ranch Hearty Elk Chili and Beans

Bring beans to a boil in 4 cups (1000 mL) of water to cover the beans, turn to simmer and continue cooking. In a skillet sauté elk until almost done. Add onion, garlic, green bell pepper. Sauté until onion is clear. Add flour and stir until flour forms paste. Add tomatoes, tomato sauce, and water. Stir until well mixed. Add remaining spices and cocoa. Bring mixture to a boil and simmer for 15 minutes. Add to cooking beans and continue cooking until beans are tender. Add water as needed during cooking. Stir often.

Elk Sirloin with Portobello Mushrooms and Soy-Lemon Marinade

In a bowl, combine the elk, scallions, soy sauce, 3 tablespoons (45 mL) of the olive oil, the lemon juice, garlic, pepper, and thyme. To marinate, cover and refrigerate 2 hours or longer.

Slice the mushroom stems and save them for another use. Slice the caps about 1/2-inch thick. Heat the remaining 2 tablespoons (30 mL) olive oil in a large skillet over medium high heat. Add the mushrooms and stir well. Sprinkle with salt and pepper and cook, stirring frequently, until the mushrooms are tender, about 5 minutes. Remove the mushrooms and any liquid from the pan and set aside. Place the pan over medium high heat and add about half the elk with any marinade that adheres to it. Separate the elk pieces so they don't steam as they cook. For rare or medium-rare, brown on all sides for about 2 minutes total. Remove from the pan and keep warm. Repeat with remaining elk. Pour off any fat remaining in the skillet, leaving any browned bits of meat. Add the beef stock and vermouth to the pan and return it to medium high heat. Stir well, scraping the bottom of the pan with a wooden spoon to dislodge the browned bits, and boil until the liquid is reduced and slightly thickened. Decrease the heat to medium or medium low. Add the mushrooms and cook for a few seconds, while stirring, then add the elk with any juices and cook briefly, continuing to stir, just until the meat is heated thoroughly. Serve immediately.

SERVES 4

1-1/2 lbs	**elk sirloins or tenderloins**	681g
	trimmed and cut into 2x1x1 strips	
1/2 cup	**scallions**	125 mL
	thinly sliced	
2 tbsp	**dark soy sauce, or regular soy sauce**	30 mL
	plus 1 teaspoon (5 mL) sugar	
5 tbsp	**extra virgin olive oil**	75 mL
	divided	
2 tbsp	**lemon juice**	30 mL
	freshly squeezed	
2	**garlic cloves**	2
	minced	
1/2 tsp	**black pepper**	2 mL
	freshly ground	
1/2 tsp	**whole dried thyme leaves**	2 mL
	crumbled	
1 lb	**Portobello mushrooms**	454 g
	salt and freshly ground black pepper	
1 cup	**rich beef stock**	250 mL
1 cup	**dry white French vermouth**	250 mL

Chef Christopher Ray and Greg Linder Medallions of Caribou Loin

SERVES 4

2 lb	**caribou loin**	908 g
3	**bacon slices**	3

MARINADE

2 tbsp	**salad oil**	30 mL
1/3 cup	**soy sauce**	75 mL
1/4 cup	**pineapple juice**	60 mL
1/3 cup	**sherry**	75 mL
8	**cloves of garlic** chopped	8
1/4 cup	**fresh ginger** chopped	60 mL
1/4 cup	**fresh chives** chopped	60 mL

SAUCE

1/4 cup	**fresh huckleberries** or lingonberries or blueberries	60 mL
1-1/2 cups	**burgundy wine**	375 mL
2 cups	**beef stock**	500 mL
1/2 cup	**sugar**	125 mL
1	**rosemary sprig**	1
1	**bag leaf**	1
1/2 tsp	**black pepper** cracked	2 mL
1/2 cup	**cold butter chunks**	125 mL

Combine all ingredients of marinade. Place marinade and loin in plastic bag and marinade overnight in refrigerator. Remove loin from marinade and brown all sides of loin in a very hot sauté pan. Place the loin in a roasting pan and set the slices of bacon on top of the roast. Roast in a 325°F (160°C) oven about 12 to 15 minutes. Remove from oven and let set for 10 to 15 minutes before slice into 1/2-inch thick medallions. Serve by pouring the sauce on the plate, and fan the medallions over the sauce.

Sauce

In a sauté pan, add burgundy wine, stock, sugar, rosemary sprig, bay leaf, and pepper. Simmer until liquid is reduced by three-quarters. Remove from heat and slowly whisk in the cold butter chunks until all have blended. Strain and add the berries.

Medallions of Caribou Loin

John Ash's Grilled Wild Boar Chops with Honey-Mustard Apricot Glaze

Glaze

In a heavy saucepan, combine the apricots and water. Bring to a boil, reduce heat, and simmer uncovered for 12 to 15 minutes or until the apricots are tender and the liquid is reduced by half. In a separate sauté pan, melt the butter and sauté the shallots until softened but not brown. Transfer the apricot mixture and the shallots to a food processor along with the vinegar, mustard, honey, salt, and white pepper, and purée until smooth. Return the mixture to the saucepan and bring to a simmer. Simmer uncovered 8 to 10 minutes or until thickened. (Glaze can be cooked and stored in the refrigerator for up to 3 weeks).

Marinate the boar chops in 1 cup (250 mL) of the glaze for several hours or overnight in the refrigerator.

Prepare a fire in a charcoal grill. Lift chops from marinade and drain briefly, reserving marinade. Place chops on a lightly greased grill 4- to 6-inches above a solid bed of medium coals. Cook, brushing occasionally with marinade and turning once, until meat near bone is no longer pink, about 4 to 5 minutes per side.

SERVES 4

8	**wild boar saddle chops**	8
	olive oil	

GLAZE

1/2 lb	**dried apricots**	113.5 g
1-1/2 cups	**water**	375 mL
2 tbsp	**unsalted butter**	30 mL
1/4 cup	**shallots** finely minced	60 mL
2/3 cup	**white wine vinegar**	150 mL
1/4 cup	**Dijon mustard**	60 mL
1/2 cup	**honey**	125 mL
1 tsp	**salt**	5 mL
1/4 tsp	**white pepper** freshly ground	1 mL

Venison Roast with Orange, Ginger and Mint Salsa

SERVES 5

1	**venison hind leg roast**	1
1/4 tsp	**salt and fresh black pepper**	1 mL
1/4 cup	**brown sugar**	60 mL
1 tsp	**olive oil**	5 mL
2 tbsp	**course mustard**	30 mL
1 tsp	**brown sugar**	5 mL

SALSA

4	**oranges** peeled and segmented	4
1/4	**red bell pepper** finely diced	1/4
3 tbsp	**lime or lemon juice**	45 mL
2 tbsp	**fresh mint** chopped	30 mL
1/4 tsp	**small chili** finely diced or 1/4 tsp (1 mL) chili powder	1 mL
2 tbsp	**virgin olive oil**	30 mL
1/2	**red onion, sweet onion, or 2 green onions** finely chopped	1/2
	pinch of sugar	

Season venison liberally with salt and black pepper and brown sugar in a lightly oiled, preheated skillet. Combine mustard, brown sugar and spread over roast. Transfer meat to a roasting dish and roast at 425°F (220°C) for 10–12 minutes. Let stand for 5 minutes before carving. To prepare salsa, combine all ingredients in a bowl. Season to taste with salt, freshly ground black pepper and a pinch of sugar. To serve, fan slices of meat on to a serving plate and accompany with a mound of salsa.

Variation

Different fruits can be used to prepare the salsa. Substitute oranges with either 1/2 fresh pineapple diced or 4 fresh peaches, diced, or 2 cups (500 mL) of canned peaches in juice, drained and diced.

Arctic Muskox Rouladen

SERVES 6

18	**muskox (top round)** 1-1/2 ounce thin slices	18
	salt and pepper to taste	
	Dijon mustard to taste	
1 cup	**ham** cut lengthwise	250 mL
1 cup	**pickle** cut lengthwise	250 mL
1 cup	**carrot** cut lengthwise	250 mL
1 tbsp	**flour**	15 mL
2 tbsp	**butter**	30 mL
1-1/4 cups	**game stock**	310 mL
3/4 cup	**red wine**	175 mL

Rub muskox slices with salt, pepper and mustard. Cut ham, pickle and carrot into strips 2-1/2 inches long and place on slices of muskox. Roll up tightly and secure with toothpicks. Dip rolls in flour and fry in butter to brown on all sides. Add stock, cover and cook for 30 minutes. Add wine and reduce, scraping bottom of pan. Season to taste.

Venison Sausage with Bread Stuffing

With a serrated bread knife, cut the bread into 1-inch cubes. Dry the cubes overnight. Sauté the onion and celery in the butter until transparent; set aside. Sauté the sausage meat and ground venison, stirring until crumbled and cooked through. In a large bowl soak the bread in as much milk as it will absorb using an entire quart if necessary. Add the sautéed onion and celery, cooked sausage, venison, parsley, salt, and pepper to taste. Mix well. Put stuffing in a well buttered casserole dish, and bake in a 375°F (190°C) oven uncovered for 1 to 1-1/2 hours until nicely browned.

SERVES 6

1	**large loaf sourdough bread**	1
3 tbsp	**butter**	45 mL
1	**onion** chopped	1
2	**celery ribs** chopped	2
1/2 lb	**bulk pork sausage** fresh	227 g
1/2 lb	**ground venison**	227 g
4 cups	**milk**	1000 mL
1/2 cup	**parsley** chopped	125 mL
	salt, pepper and thyme to taste	

Cougar Ranch Buffalo Roast

Combine wine, bay leaves, minced onion, celery, parsley, and oregano. Pour over meat, cover, and marinate overnight. Take meat from marinade and reserve liquid. Dredge meat in seasoned flour. Heat oil in Dutch oven and brown meat on all sides. Combine marinade and tomato sauce and pour over meat. Bake 3 to 4 hours at 300°F (150°C) or until meat is tender.

Remove roast from oven and slice, laying slices in shallow baking dish. Spoon sauce from Dutch oven over meat. Crumble bacon and sprinkle over top; arrange onion rings over all. Return to oven for 15 minutes.

SERVES 8 – 10

4–6 lb	**buffalo haunch**	2–3 kg
1-1/2 cups	**burgundy wine**	375 mL
3/4 cup	**flour**	175 mL
1/2 tsp	**salt** optional	2 mL
1/8 tsp	**pepper**	0.5 mL
2	**bay leaves**	2
1 cup	**onion** finely minced	250 mL
1/2 cup	**celery** minced	125 mL
2 tbsp	**parsley flakes**	30 mL
2 tbsp	**oregano**	30 mL
4 tbsp	**oil**	60 mL
1 cup	**tomato sauce**	250 mL
4	**strips of bacon** crisp	4
1	**small onion** sliced and separated into rings	1

Savory Wild Boar Roast

SERVES 4

5 lbs.	**wild boar roast**	2.3 kg
3	**large garlic cloves** chopped	3
1	**large onion** chopped	1
2 tbsp	**parsley flakes**	30 mL
1/2	**lemon with rind**	1/2
1/2	**tangerine with rind**	1/2
1 tbsp	**each cilantro,** **rosemary, oregano, and thyme**	60 mL
1 cup	**white wine**	250 mL
1/2 cup	**soy sauce**	125 mL
1/3 cup	**olive oil**	75 mL

In a large bowl combine garlic, onion, parsley flakes, citrus (squeezed and adding only half to bowl). Add herbs together and combine well. Add wine, soy sauce and oil. Rinse meat under cool tap water and pat dry. Place in large baking dish and pour marinade over the top. Cover and refrigerate up to 24 hours turning occasionally. Place meat in a roasting pan and roast at 325°F (160°C) for about 2 hours or until meat thermometer reads 170 degrees.

Savory Wild Boar Roast

Wild Game Chili Con Carne

Drain the beans, cover with fresh cold water, bring to a boil and cook for at least 30 minutes. Set aside. Meanwhile, heat the oil in a deep pan, put in the ground venison and cook till lightly browned; sprinkle over with paprika and chili powder. Add the onion, garlic and chili peppers if using and fry till golden brown. Stir in the carrots, leeks, tomatoes and beans with their cooking liquid; crumble in the bouillon cube, add the herbs, cover and simmer gently for 35 minutes. Remove the bay leaves and season to taste with salt. Serve immediately with crusty French bread.

SERVES 2

1-1/2 cups	**dried red kidney or pinto beans**	375 mL
	soaked overnight in cold water to cover	
1/4 cup	**olive oil**	60 mL
1 lb	**ground venison**	454 g
1 tbsp	**paprika**	15 mL
1 tsp	**chili powder**	5 mL
4	**onions**	4
	peeled and finely chopped	
2	**cloves of garlic**	2
	peeled and finely chopped	
2	**red or green chili peppers**	2
	deseeded and finely (optional)	
2	**carrots**	2
	peeled and diced	
2	**leeks**	2
	washed, trimmed and sliced	
2 cups	**canned tomatoes**	500 mL
1	**beef bouillon cube**	1
1 tsp	**dried thyme**	5 mL
3	**bay leaves**	3
	salt and pepper to taste	

Roast Tenderloin of Buffalo with Cranberry Chipotle Sauce

Rinse tenderloin under cool tap water and pat dry. Wrap with bacon and secure with toothpicks. Roast at 425°F (220°C) for 40 minutes per pound.

Sauce
Combine all ingredients in a saucepan and mix thoroughly. Simmer for 20 minutes then purée. Serve buffalo sliced with sauce on top.

SERVES 10 – 12

5–7 lb	**buffalo tenderloin**	2.3–3.2 kg
1 lb	**apple wood bacon**	454 g
	sliced	

SAUCE

4	**chipotle peppers**	4
	de-seeded and diced	
1	**small onion**	1
	diced	
1	**red bell pepper**	1
	diced	
1	**bottle dark beer**	1
2	**cloves garlic**	2
	minced	
1 cup	**brown sugar**	250 mL
1-1/2 cups	**cider vinegar**	375 mL
1/2 cup	**tomato paste**	125 mL
1/4 cup	**molasses**	60 mL
4 cups	**cranberries**	1000 mL

Alisal Guest Ranch Braised Brisket with Danse Skjold Pale Ale

SERVES 8 – 10

3 lbs	**game brisket**	1.4 kg
	salt and pepper to taste	
3 tbsp	**olive oil**	45 mL
6	**fresh thyme sprigs**	6
2	**bay leaves**	2
2	**onion** medium-sized, diced	2
1/4	**stalk celery** diced	1/4
6	**carrots** diced	6
8	**garlic cloves** chopped	8
1	**celery root** medium-sized. diced	1
2	**small white turnips** diced	2
2	**small rutabagas** diced	2
4	**bottles of Danse Skjold Pale Ale**	4
4 tbsp	**tomato paste**	60 mL
8 cups	**game stock**	2000 mL

Preheat oven to 325°F (160°C). Season brisket with salt and pepper. Heat olive oil in a heavy-bottomed casserole. Brown brisket on both sides, about 4 to 5 minutes each side. Place brisket on platter. Add onions, garlic, carrots, celery, celery root, turnips, rutabagas, bay leaves, and thyme to casserole and sauté for about 5 minutes. Deglaze vegetables with ale; reduce by half. Add game stock and tomato paste; season to taste with salt and pepper. Add brisket and juices from the platter to the casserole. Cook in oven for 2-1/2 hours (2 hours covered, 1/2 hour uncovered).

Borga's Hideaway Southwest Prime Rib

SERVES 8 – 10

1	**prime rib roast** elk, deer, antelope or moose	1
1 cup	**stone-ground mustard**	250 mL
1/4 cup	**balsamic vinegar**	60 mL
3 tbsp	**coarse ground pepper**	45 mL
1 tbsp	**salt**	15 mL

Mix together mustard, vinegar, salt and pepper and rub onto meat, coating meat thickly. Roast 350°F (175°C) for 15 minutes per pound. Let rest for 15 minutes, then carve and enjoy!

Venison Steaks with Blueberry Sauce

Combine brown sugar and malt vinegar in a medium-sized saucepan. Stir over low heat to dissolve sugar. Add blueberries and white wine. Simmer for about 10 to 12 minutes. Just before sauce is cooked, season steaks with black pepper. Heat oil in a heavy-based skillet. Cook steaks over high heat for 3 minutes each side or until meat is browned and cooked to medium-rare. While steaks cook, make a paste with cornstarch and water or port and add to sauce, stirring over heat until boiling. Adjust seasoning to taste. Slice steaks, and fan onto serving plates. Spoon sauce around and garnish with fresh berries and sprig of thyme or oregano.

Variation

A variety of different fruits can be used to prepare the salsa. Substitute oranges for either 1/2 fresh pineapple, diced or 4 fresh peaches, diced, or 2 cups (500 mL) of peaches in juice, drained and diced. You can substitute any type of berry in place of blueberries for sauce in this recipe.

SERVES 4

4	venison hind leg steaks	4
2 tbsp	brown sugar	30 mL
2 tbsp	malt vinegar	30 mL
1-1/2 cups	frozen blueberries	375 mL
1/2 cup	white wine	125 mL
	salt and pepper to taste	
	freshly ground black pepper	
1 tbsp	olive oil	15 mL
1-1/2 tsp	cornstarch	7 mL
1 tbsp	port or water	15 mL

A Bit of the Wild Mexican Lasagna

Sauté meat in heavy skillet, stir in taco seasoning. First layer–place enough tortillas to cover bottom of the pan and a little up the sides. Second layer–cover with half of the meat mixture and a little cheese. Third layer–spread refried beans, green peppers, taco sauce. Fourth layer–place the remainder of the meat. Fifth layer–top with salsa then cheese. Bake at 350°F (175°C) until all mixtures are heated and cheese is melted.

SERVES 8

1 lb	ground venison	454 g
1/4 cup	taco seasoning	60 mL
1 pkg	8-inch flour tortillas	1 pkg
1-3/4 cups	refried beans	425 mL
3 cups	mozzarella cheese and Monterey Jack combined	750 mL
3/4 cup	salsa	175 mL
	green pepper to taste finely chopped	
3/4 cup	taco sauce	175 mL

Marengo Casserole

SERVES 4 – 6

3 lbs	**venison roast**	1.4 kg
	or game of your choice	
2	**recipes Marinade for Game**	2
	(see page 85)	
1-1/2 lb	**sliced salt pork**	227 g
1-1/2 cups	**water**	375 mL
1 lb	**small onions**	454 g
1 lb	**small fresh mushrooms**	454 g
	butter	
10 oz	**can consommé**	300 mL
1 cup	**tomato sauce**	250 mL
1/4 cup	**flour**	60 mL
1/4 cup	**water**	60 mL
	salt and fresh ground pepper to taste	
1 tbsp	**dry sherry**	15 mL
1 tbsp	**brandy**	15 mL

Place the venison in a shallow pan, and then pour the marinade over the venison. Refrigerate for 12 to 24 hours, turning occasionally. Drain off the marinade, then strain and reserve. Wipe the venison dry and place on a rack in a roasting pan. Wash the salt pork and place over the venison. Pour the water into the pan, then add 1 cup (250 mL) of the reserved marinade. Roast in a preheated oven 325°F (160°C) oven for 2 hours or until done, basting with the pan drippings occasionally. Peel the onions and cook in boiling, salted water until tender, then drain. Sauté the mushrooms in a small amount of butter until lightly browned. Remove the venison from the broiling pan and place on a cutting board. Let cool for 20 to 30 minutes, cut into cubes. The remaining salt pork rind may be discarded or cut into thin strips and served with the venison roast.Place the venison in a large skillet and add the onions, mushrooms, consommé, tomato sauce and 1 cup (250 mL) of the pan drippings. Combine the flour with 1/4 cup (60 mL) of water and mix until smooth, then stir into the venison mixture. Season with salt and pepper, then add the sherry and brandy. Simmer stirring frequently, for 15 minutes or until thickened. This may be made the day before serving and reheated.

Rum-Spiced Elk Chops

In a large skillet heat oil and add onion, jalapeños, garlic, thyme, cinnamon, nutmeg, cloves and bay leaf. Cook, stirring frequently until mixture is a golden brown. Increase heat and stir in rum, lime juice and salt. Cook for about 2 minutes. Remove from heat and discard bay leaf. Allow marinade to cool completely.

Rinse elk chops in cool tap water and pat dry. Place in a shallow dish and spoon half of the marinade over the chops. Turn chops over and add remaining marinade. Cover and refrigerate up to 4 hours. Heat grill to medium heat. Place chops directly on grill. Grill chops covered for 5 to 6 minutes on each side or until desired doneness.

SERVES 4

4	**elk loin chops** bone in	4
1 tbsp	**oil**	15 mL
1	**medium onion** finely chopped	1
2	**jalapeño peppers** seeded and finely chopped	2
4	**garlic cloves** minced	4
1/2 tsp	**dried thyme leaves**	2 mL
1/2 tsp	**cinnamon**	2 mL
1/8 tsp	**ground nutmeg**	0.5 mL
1	**bay leaf**	1
1/4 cup	**dark rum**	60 mL
2 tbsp	**lime juice**	30 mL
1/4 tsp	**salt**	1 mL

Rum-Spiced Elk Chops

The Riverfront Plantation Inn Portobello Buffalo Tenderloin

SERVES 4 – 6

1-1/2 lbs	**buffalo tenderloin** trimmed of fat and silver skin	681 g
2 tbsp	**butter**	30 mL
2	**garlic cloves** minced	2
1/2 cup	**green onion** sliced	125 mL
3	**Portobello mushroom caps** sliced	3
1/2 cup	**red wine**	125 mL
	garlic salt to taste	
	fresh ground pepper to taste	
2	**bacon slices**	2

Melt butter in skillet, sauté garlic and onion 1 minute, add mushrooms and heat through. Add wine and cook until all liquid has reduced. Butterfly tenderloin and sprinkle with garlic salt and pepper. Stuff with mushroom mixture, secure with toothpicks and place in roasting pan cut side down. Sprinkle outside with garlic salt and pepper, wrap with bacon. Roast at 350°F (175°C) degrees, approximately 30 minutes or to desired degree of doneness. Buffalo is best medium-rare to rare.

Balsamic Glazed Rack of Venison

SERVES 4

2	**venison racks** 4 chops each	2
1-1/4 lbs		568 g
1 tbsp	**canola oil**	15 mL

GLAZE

1/4 cup	**balsamic vinegar**	60 mL
2 tbsp	**olive oil**	30 mL
1-1/2 tbsp	**ketchup**	22.5 mL
1 tbsp	**Worcestershire sauce**	15 mL
1/2 tbsp	**coarsely ground pepper**	7.5 mL
3/4 tsp	**kosher salt**	4 mL

In a bowl, combine the vinegar, olive oil, ketchup, Worcestershire sauce, pepper and salt. Preheat oven to 450°F (230°C). In an ovenproof skillet, heat the canola oil until shimmering. Set the venison racks bone side up in the skillet. Sear them over high heat, turning once until browned, about 1-1/2 minutes per side. Put the skillet in the oven and roast for about 20 minutes, brushing racks 3 times with the glaze, until the meat is rare to medium-rare. Cover with foil and let rest for 10 minutes. Season with salt and pepper. Add the remaining glaze to the skillet and bring to a boil over high heat, stirring to scrape up the browned bits. Cut the venison into chops and serve with the sauce.

Grilled Buffalo Steaks Marinated in Red Wine

Marinade

Place the olive oil and garlic in a small bowl. Slowly add the red wine, whisk all the while with a wire whisk to form an emulsion. Add the pepper; mix well. (Marinade can be stored in a covered container in the refrigerator for up to 2 weeks). Place the steaks in a non-aluminum pan and pour the marinade over, turning to coat each piece evenly. Marinate the steaks for at least 6 hours or overnight, turning several times.

Drain steaks from marinade. Place steaks on barbecue grill 6 inches above a medium-hot fire. Cook about 2 to 3 minutes per side, until medium-rare. Remove from heat and let stand 5 minutes before serving.

SERVES 4		
6	**New York Strip buffalo steaks**	6

MARINADE		
1-1/2 cups	**green or gold-colored extra-virgin olive oil**	375 mL
3	**garlic cloves** minced	3
3/4 cup	**dry red wine**	175 mL
1 tsp	**black pepper** fresh ground	5 mL

Grilled Buffalo Steaks Marinade in Red Wine

Venison Roast Marinated in Buttermilk

This is a good recipe for an older or possibly tough piece of venison. Larding, long marinating and slow, moist cooking will make for nice, tender meat.

SERVES 8 – 10

4-5 lbs	**venison leg roast** trim off all fat and membrane (Lard roast, rub well with spices)	1.8- 2.3 kg

RUB

1 tbsp	**black pepper** coarse ground	15 mL
1 tsp	**red chili pepper** ground	10 mL
1 tsp	**thyme**	5 mL
1 tsp	**sage**	5 mL
1 tbsp	**vinegar**	15 mL

Let roast sit a couple hours with spices on, then marinate.

MARINADE

4	**onions** sliced	4
4-5	**bay leaves**	4-5
6	**garlic cloves** crushed	6
1 tsp	**whole black peppercorns**	5 mL
1	**small stick of cinnamon**	1
8 cups	**buttermilk**	2000 mL

ROAST

2	**bottles good beer or cider**	2
2	**onions** diced	2
2	**apples** sliced	2
1	**sweet potato** diced	1

Rub

Combine all the ingredients in the rub and let roast sit a couple hours with spices on, then marinate.

Combine marinade ingredients and mix well. Marinate venison roast in refrigerator for 2 to 3 days, turning occasionally. Drain roast, discard marinade. Brown roast well in a bit of bacon grease in a Dutch oven. Drain grease and add a bottle of good beer or cider. Cover and bake slowly, 325°F (160°C) for an hour or two. Add a couple onions, carrots, a couple apples and a sweet potato or two. Add more beer, cider or water to maintain liquid level. Continue to roast until vegetables and roast are tender.

Chef Alan Heron Rabbit Dijonnaise

Combine marinade ingredients in a large shallow bowl. Stir to blend. Add boned rabbit legs and turn in marinade to evenly coat. Refrigerate for 1 hour. Remove from marinade and pat dry with paper toweling. Reserve marinade mixture. Heat olive oil in a large frying pan. Add onion and garlic and sauté until soft and clear. Add rabbit legs and sauté on all sides over medium heat for 8 to 10 minutes. Remove rabbit from the pan and set aside. Whisk in mustard, Worcestershire sauce, salt and pepper to taste. Whisk in 1/2 tablespoon (7.5 mL) of flour. Cook for a couple of minutes. Strain marinade and add 1/2 cup (125 mL) to the pan. Whisk until smooth. Whisk in cream and remaining strained marinade. Add rabbit. Cover and simmer for 20 to 25 minutes until rabbit is tender and sauce coats a metal spoon.

Meanwhile, cook linguine as directed on package. Drain and place on a large platter forming a nest of noodles. Place rabbit legs into the nest of noodles and drizzle with pan juices. Serve at once.

SERVES 2 – 3

6	**rabbit legs** boned	6
1/4 cup	**flour** divided	60 mL
2 tbsp	**olive oil**	30 mL
1	**medium onion** finely chopped	1
1	**large garlic clove** crushed	1
1 tsp	**Dijon mustard**	5 mL
	dash of Worcestershire sauce	
	salt and freshly ground black pepper	
1/3 cup	**whipping cream**	75 mL
1 lb	**wild rice linguine**	454 g

MARINADE

2 cups	**vegetable stock**	500 mL
1/2 cup	**dry white wine**	125 mL
1 tbsp	**Dijon mustard**	15 mL
1	**large garlic clove** crushed	1
2	**dashes Worcestershire sauce**	2
	pinch of fresh or dried thyme	
	salt and freshly ground black pepper	

Antelope or Venison Medallions with Brown Sauce

SERVES 4

1 lb	**venison medallions**	454 g

MARINADE

2 tbsp	**B & B liqueur**	30 mL
1 tbsp	**light olive oil**	15 mL
	with a dash of toasted sesame oil	
1	**small shallot**	1
	minced	
1	**clove of garlic**	1
	peeled and minced	
1/8 tsp	**sea salt**	0.5 mL
	freshly ground	
1/8 tsp	**black pepper**	0.5 mL
	freshly ground	

SAUCE

1	**small shallot**	1
	minced	
1	**garlic clove**	1
	peeled and minced	
1 cup	**beef stock**	250 mL
2 tbsp	**sour cream**	30 mL
1/4 cup	**B & B liqueur**	60 mL

Marinade

In a medium bowl combine all the marinade ingredients, place the meat in the marinade, and refrigerate for about 2 hours.

Pour the oil into a heavy-based skillet on medium heat. Remove meat from marinade and dry well with paper towel. Sear medallions in skillet for about 3 minutes per side. Remove from the pan.

Sauce

In the same skillet on medium heat, fry the shallot and garlic for 2 minutes. Return the medallions to the pan, add the liqueur, and flambé. When the flames have subsided, remove the meat and keep warm in the oven. To the same skillet, add the stock, increase the heat to high, and boil until it is reduced to about 3/4 cup (175 mL), about 5 minutes. In a small bowl, mix 1 tablespoon (15 mL) of the reduced stock into the sour cream, then stir the mixture into the hot sauce. Keep warm but do not let boil. Pool the sauce onto warm plates and place 2 medallions in each pool.

Garnish with cooked shrimp.

Antelope or Venison Medallions with Brown Sauce

Cougar Ranch Black Bean Buffalo Chili

Rinse beans thoroughly in cold water. In a large, heavy saucepan, heat the beans and water to boiling and boil 3 minutes. Remove from heat, cover and let stand for 1 hour. Add enough water, if necessary, to cover beans and heat to boiling again. Reduce heat, cover and simmer for 1-1/2 hours. Beans should be tender. Remove beans and liquid from saucepan and set aside, reserving the liquid. Brown the buffalo and onion in the saucepan. Add green pepper, red chili pepper, chili powder, and garlic powder. Add tomatoes and liquid, crushing each tomato, as it is needed. Add tomato sauce and mushrooms. Add beans and liquid in which they were cooked to meat mixture. Heat chili to boiling, reduce heat, and simmer about 2 hours, stirring occasionally.

SERVES 6 – 8

1/2 cup	**dried black turtle beans**	125 mL
1/2 cup	**dried red kidney beans**	125 mL
2 cups	**water**	500 mL
1 lb	**ground buffalo meat**	454 g
1	**small onion** diced	1
1	**small green bell pepper** diced	1
1	**dried red chili pepper** crumbled into small pieces	1
2 tsp	**chili powder**	10 mL
1/2 tsp	**garlic powder**	2 mL
1/2 cup	**fresh mushrooms** sliced	125 mL
7 cups	**whole canned tomatoes** including liquid	1750 mL
2 cups	**tomato sauce**	500 mL

Buffalo Top Sirloin with Dijon Cream Sauce

SERVES 4

2-16 oz	**sirloin steaks** 3/4-inch thickness	2-454 g
1/2 cup	**Dijon mustard** divided	125 mL
4 tsp	**black peppercorns** ground coarsely, separated	20 mL
2 tbsp	**oil**	30 mL
1/2 cup	**shallots** minced	125 mL
1	**clove garlic** minced	1
1 cup	**beef broth**	250 mL
1/4 cup	**whipping cream**	60 mL
1/4 cup	**brandy**	60 mL

Rinse steaks under cool tap water and pat dry. Dust each side lightly with garlic powder, salt and coarse black pepper. Spread 2 tablespoons (30 mL) mustard on one side of steak and dust with 1 teaspoon (5 mL) of peppercorns and press into steaks. Turn and repeat process. Heat oil in skillet. Add steaks and cook until desired doneness about 5 minutes on each side for medium-rare. When done remove and keep warm. Add shallots and garlic to skillet. Sauté for about 15 to 20 seconds. Stir in broth, cream, brandy and 1 tablespoon (15 mL) of mustard. Bring to a low boil and thicken. About 2 minutes. Serve steaks topped with cream sauce.

Buffalo Top Sirloin with Dijon Cream Sauce

Rio Grande Salami

If you think making salami is mysterious
and best left to commercial meat processors
think again. You can easily make this in
your kitchen.

Mix all ingredients in a non-metal bowl.
Refrigerate for 3 days, thoroughly mixing
each day with hands. On the fourth day
divide mixture into 5 parts. Knead and form
into long thin logs about 12 inches long.
Place logs on cookie sheet and bake at
around 175°F (80°C) degrees. After 5 hours,
turn logs over and cook 5 more hours.
Remove from oven and roll in paper towels
to remove excess grease. Cool, wrap in foil,
and keep in refrigerator.

SERVES 6 – 8

4 lbs	**ground venison**	1.8 kg
2	**yellow onions** diced	2
1/2 lb	**ground beef suet**	227 g
2 tsp	**black pepper**	10 mL
1/2 tsp	**garlic powder**	2 mL
2 cups	**tomato sauce**	500 mL
5 tsp	**salt**	25 mL
2-1/2 tsp	**Liquid Smoke**	12 mL
1-1/2 tsp	**small red chilies**	7 mL

Roast Tenderloin of Buffalo with Wild Mushrooms

Rinse tenderloin under cool tap water and
pat dry. Place roast in a roasting pan and
baste with some of the butter. Season with
black pepper. Place in hot oven 450°F (230°C)
for about 15 minutes. Reduce heat to 350°F
(175°C) and roast until meat is medium-rare
or medium. In a skillet pour in remaining
butter and sauté onions, garlic and
mushrooms together until tender. When
roast is done, remove and keep warm. Pour
off drippings into a saucepan and add
Cognac. Simmer stirring to blend then add
mushroom mixture. Serve sauce over meat
slices.

SERVES 8 –10

5-7 lb	**buffalo tenderloin**	2.3 -3.2 kg
1 tsp	**coarse black pepper**	5 mL
3/4 cup	**butter** melted, divided	175 mL
1-1/2 cups	**onion** sliced thin	375 mL
1	**clove garlic** minced	1
1-1/2 cups	**mushrooms** fresh	375 mL
1/4 cup	**Cognac**	60 mL

Margarita Venison Steak with Fresh Orange Salsa

SERVES 8

8	**venison steaks**	8
2/3 cups	**pure orange juice**	150 mL
1/2 cup	**tequila**	125 mL
1/3 cup	**fresh lime juice**	75 mL
2 tbsp	**olive oil**	30 mL
2 tbsp	**fresh ginger** chopped	30 mL
1 tsp	**garlic** minced	5 mL
1 tsp	**salt**	5 mL
1 tsp	**dried oregano leaves** crushed	5 mL
1/4 tsp	**red pepper** crushed	1 mL

ORANGE SALSA

2	**oranges** peeled and chopped	2
1	**small red onion** chopped	1
1	**jalapeño pepper** seeded and chopped	1
2 tbsp	**fresh lime juice**	30 mL
2 tbsp	**olive oil**	30 mL
1/2 tsp	**salt**	2 mL
1/2 tsp	**dried oregano leaves** crushed	2 mL

Marinade

Combine orange juice, tequila, lime juice, oil, ginger, garlic, salt, oregano and pepper. Place steaks and marinade in a plastic bag. Close bag and refrigerate for 6 hours or overnight. Remove steaks from marinade and discard marinade. Grill or charbroil steaks to desired doneness. On a carving board, slice steaks thin and arrange on a serving plate. Garnish with cilantro and lemon and lime wedges. Serve with orange salsa.

Orange Salsa

Combine all ingredient in a glass bowl and chill for at least 2 hours. Serve with steak.

Margarita Venison Steak with Fresh Orange Salsa

Cider-Simmered Buffalo Roast

Heat oil in wide nonstick frying pan over medium-high heat; add roast and brown well on all sides. Meanwhile, in a large electric slow cooker, combine onions, celery, and garlic; sprinkle with allspice, ginger, and pepper. In a small bowl, mix cider and molasses. Place roast on top of onion mixture in slow cooker; pour in cider mixture. Cover and cook at low heat setting until buffalo is very tender when pierced, about 9 hours.

Lift roast to a warm platter and keep warm. Skim and discard fat from cooking liquid, if necessary; then blend in cornstarch mixture. Increase heat to high; cover and cook stirring until sauce is thickened. Season to taste with salt. Serve by discarding string from roast, then slice across the grain. Spoon some of the sauce over meat; sprinkle with parsley. Serve remaining sauce in bowl to add over noodles.

SERVES 8 – 10

4 lb	**buffalo roast**	1.8 kg
	boned, rolled, tied and trimmed of fat	
2	**onions**	2
	cut into eighths	
1	**celery stalk**	1
	thinly sliced	
2	**garlic cloves**	2
	minced or pressed	
1 tsp	**ground allspice**	5 mL
1/2 tsp	**ground ginger**	2 mL
1/4 tsp	**fresh ground pepper**	1 mL
1 cup	**apple cider**	250 mL
	or apple juice	
2 tbsp	**light molasses**	30 mL
2 tbsp	**cornstarch**	30 mL
	blended with equal amount of cold water	
	salt to taste	
	chopped parsley to taste	
	cooked noodles	
	amount depends on number of guests	

Cider-Simmered Buffalo Roast

The Farm House Venison Sausage Balls

SERVES 3 – 4

1-1/2 lbs	**ground venison**	681 g
1/2 cup	**dry bread crumbs**	125 mL
1	**egg** beaten	1
1 tsp	**salt**	5 mL
1/2 cup	**mashed potatoes**	125 mL
1/2 tsp	**brown sugar**	2 mL
1/4 tsp	**fresh black pepper**	1 mL
1/4 tsp	**allspice**	1 mL
1/4 tsp	**nutmeg**	1 mL
1/8 tsp	**cloves**	0.5 mL
1/8 tsp	**ginger**	0.5 mL
1/4 cup	**melted butter**	60 mL

Mix all ingredients except butter in bowl. Shape into 1-inch balls. Brown in butter in skillet, turning frequently. Cook covered over low heat for 15 minutes. Garnish with parsley, lemon and orange slices.

The Farm House Venison Sausage Balls

Sticky Bones

Combine vinegar, honey, Worcestershire, ketchup, salt, mustard, paprika, pepper and garlic in saucepan. Cover, bring to boil, reduce heat, and simmer 20 minutes. Place ribs in a single layer in baking pan, cover with hot marinade, and let stand 1 hour. Drain off marinade, set aside, then bake ribs at 325°F (160°C) for 1 hour, turning and basting often with marinade.

SERVES 6 – 8

1 cup	**vinegar**	250 mL
1/2 cup	**honey**	125 mL
2 tbsp	**Worcestershire sauce**	30 mL
1/2 cup	**ketchup**	125 mL
1 tsp	**salt**	5 mL
1 tsp	**dry mustard**	5 mL
1 tsp	**paprika**	5 mL
1/4 tsp	**black pepper**	1 mL
1	**clove of garlic** minced	1
4 lbs	**rib bones, venison, elk or moose** any wild game bones can be used	1.8 kg

Saltimboca

This is a classic Italian recipe and a great way to cook a tender piece of venison. For the showman, this is a natural for tableside chafing dish presentation, complete with flames and the most wonderful aroma imaginable.

For two people, you will need two thin 4–5 ounce pieces of venison, the sirloin or a tender slice of leg are ideal. With a meat hammer, carefully flatten the meat until it is very thin. Try for a roughly square shape when you are done. On each piece of meat, place a couple very thin slices of Italian prosciutto ham. On these, put a thin slice of good mozzarella cheese, about 1/8 inch thick. Roll each slice of venison, jellyroll fashion, tucking the ends in neatly. Tie in a couple places with butcher's twine so they will hold together. The Saltimboca can be prepared to this point well ahead of when they will be needed. Just before serving, heat a heavy skillet or chafing dish. Flame the wine; when flames go out add butter. Cook until reaching desired doneness.

SERVES 2

2 tbsp	**butter**	30 mL
2	**thin pieces of venison**	2
1/4 cup	**real Italian dry Marsala wine**	60 mL
2 tbsp	**butter**	30 mL
	prosciutto ham thin slices	
	mozzarella cheese thin slices	

Bluebonnet Venison Farms Herbed Venison Roast

SERVES 8 – 10

2-4 lb	**venison shoulder roast**	1-2 kg
1 tbsp	**dry Provençal herbs** (equal amounts of basil, thyme, rosemary, oregano, sagem marjoram)	15 mL
1 lb	**thick-sliced bacon**	454 g
1 cup	**Raisinberry Relish**	250 mL

RAISINBERRY RELISH

2-1/4 cups	**golden raisins**	560 mL
2 cups	**orange juice**	500 mL
1 cup	**water**	250 mL
1/2 cup	**sugar**	125 mL
1/4 cup	**lemon juice**	60 mL
3 cups	**fresh or frozen cranberries**	750 mL
1 tbsp	**orange peel**	15 mL

Roast

Rub roast with herbs. Wrap roast with overlapping bacon slices; tie securely. Place on rack in shallow roasting pan. Baste with puréed Raisinberry Relish. Place in preheated 500°F (260°C) oven. Reduce heat to 400°F (205°C); roast 15 minutes per pound. Serve rare with additional Raisinberry Relish.

Raisinberry Relish

In large saucepan combine raisins, orange juice, water, sugar and lemon juice. Bring to boil over high heat, stirring to dissolve sugar. Reduce heat and simmer 10 minutes. Add cranberries and orange peel. Return to boil; simmer about 10 minutes until liquid barely covers solid ingredients. Cool. Store, refrigerated in covered container up to one month.

Taste of the Wild Steak Diane

SERVES 4

4-8oz.	**strip loin steaks**	4-227 g
	salt and fresh pepper to taste	
2 tbsp	**vegetable oil**	30 mL
4 tbsp	**unsalted butter**	60 mL
2	**medium-size shallots** finely chopped	2
3 tbsp	**port wine**	45 mL
1/2 cup	**whipping cream**	125 mL
1 tsp	**Worcestershire sauce**	5 mL
4 tbsp	**Stilton cheese** crumbled	60 mL
	finely sliced chives for garnish	

Season the steaks with salt and pepper. Melt the oil and butter together in heavy skillet. When very hot fry each side until medium-rare. Remove the steaks and cover with foil and place in warm pan.

Add shallots to the frying pan, sauté briefly and deglaze the pan with port wine. Add the whipping cream, Worcestershire sauce and reduce until sauce is thickened. Add cheese and any meat juices that have drained off the steaks to the skillet. Serve with slices of chives.

Venison Tenderloins with Brandy Sauce

Trim and discard any fat or silver membrane on tenderloins. Rinse meat and pat dry. Cut across the grain into 4 equal pieces. Coat slices with flour, shake off excess. In a large frying pan over high heat, melt butter in olive oil. When oil in frying pan is very hot, add meat and sauté on both sides, 4 to 6 minutes total (meat will be medium-rare). Add brandy and set aflame (not beneath a vent or near flammables). Shake pan until flame dies. Transfer meat to a small warm platter; keep warm. To pan, add shallots and thyme leaves. Reduce heat to medium high; stir often until shallots just begin to brown, about 2 minutes. Add broth, cream, and peppercorns. Boil on high heat, stirring often until reduced by half, about 2 minutes. Drain any juices from meat into pan; taste sauce and add lemon juice to give a mild tang. Spoon sauce around meat, garnish platter with thyme sprigs, and serve with salt and pepper to taste.

SERVES 4

1 lb	**venison tenderloins**	454 g
1-1/2 tsp	**butter or margarine**	7 mL
1-3/4 tsp	**olive oil**	7 mL
2 tbsp	**brandy**	30 mL
1/4 cup	**shallots** minced	60 mL
1/5 tsp	**thyme leaves** fresh or dried	2 mL
1/4 cup	**chicken broth**	60 mL
1/4 cup	**whipping cream**	60 mL
2 tsp	**canned green peppercorns** drained	10 mL
2 tsp	**lemon juice** optional	10 mL
	fresh thyme sprigs	
	salt and pepper to taste	

Bluebonnet Venison Farms Herbed Venison Roast

sausages

Make unbelievably delicious jerky at a fraction of the cost. Making Jerky is a great way to use up them honkers! The mild taste of summer sausage bologna you will always remember. Salami a little spicier with a hint of garlic! Country Style Sausages, just wonderful now you can enjoy the great maple taste of country style sausages prepared fresh in your own kitchen. Pepperoni, everybody's favorite for a spicy taste.

Corned Meat – Venison, Elk, Turkey

This is one of easiest ways to make special treats for dinner. Not only is it easy, but it also takes no special equipment such as grinders and sausage stuffer tubes —and no casings are needed either.

The cure being used (sodium nitrate) has the ability to change the flavor of the meat that is being cured. Try different meats and you will agree. "Why didn't I know about this sooner?" Very easy, very good. You can't go wrong.

Venison and elk come out as remarkably good as any corned beef you ever bought at the market. Use any cut of the meat: corned beef is usually made from the brisket and corned wild game can be made from any piece of meat that is trimmed up into a nice clean shape. I use the arm part of the front leg of deer and find it excellent as corned meat. Turkey thighs may also be used and taste remarkably the same as corned beef.

10 cups	**water**	2500mL
1-1/2 oz	**powder cure**	56 g
1 tsp	**garlic juice or crushed fresh garlic**	5 mL
1/2 cup	**plain salt**	125 mL
1-1/2 oz	**powdered dextrose**	56 g
1/4 cup	**good pickling salt**	60 mL

Method

Mix all dry ingredients, except the pickling spices, and fully dissolve into the water. Then add in the pickling spices. Place into glass gallon jug and add your meat of choice. You can do several pieces of meat at once. Put into the brine and place into refrigerator until done: less than two inches of meat thickness cures for 3 days, 3 to 4 inches of meat thickness cures in 4 to 5 days, etc.

Cook one fresh for dinner and place the others in zipper freezer bags and freeze for another time. Corned meat is cooked until done and tender in boiling water.

Corned Meat – Venison, Elk, Turkey

Variation
Take this same brine without the pickling spices and you can make a nice piece of meat very similar to a good ham. After being cured properly in the brine, simply cook in your smoker until done. The brine will take care of the flavor and the texture; your smoker will get it fully cooked. Cook the meat to a 175° internal temperature.

Using a little common sense and initiative, some very good meals can be created from this one idea.

Venison Sausage

5 lbs	**boneless fresh venison trimmings**	2270 g
2 lbs	**fresh pork fat**	908 g
2	**large onions** chopped	2
4	**garlic cloves**	4
2	**bay leaves**	2
2 tsp	**freshly ground black pepper**	10 mL
2 tsp	**salt and pepper to taste**	10 mL
1/2 tsp	**dried red pepper flakes**	2 mL
1 tsp	**paprika**	5 mL
3 tbsp	**minced fresh parsley**	45 mL
1 tbsp	**chopped fresh thyme**	15 mL
3 yd	**sheep casings**	.9 m

Put the venison and pork fat through a sausage grinder twice. Grind the onions, garlic and bay leaves and mix with the ground meat in a large bowl. Sprinkle with the remaining seasonings and mix well. Pan fry a small patty of the sausage mixture to test for seasoning and adjust as needed.

Cut the sausage casings into 3-foot lengths and wash by hooking one end to the kitchen faucet and flushing with cold water. Fill the casings with the sausage mixture, using the small tube on the sausage stuffer. To make links, twist the casings every 4 inches. Tie at each end and refrigerate overnight to let the flavors blend.

The sausage may smoked in a home smoker according to the manufacturer's instructions, or roasted in a 350°F (175°C) oven for 20–30 minutes. Cooked sausages freeze well.

Wild Boar Sausage

Grind wild boar meat and add seasonings. Put mixture through sausage grinder twice. Stuff into sausage skins (skins may be purchased from your butcher) and smoke continuously for 4 days.

9 lbs	**lean ground wild boar meat**	4086 g
1 lb	**fat boar meat**	454 g
4 tbsp	**salt**	60 mL
1/2 tsp	**ginger**	2 mL
1 tsp	**sage**	5 mL
1 tbsp	**black pepper**	15 mL
1 tbsp	**red pepper**	15 mL

Jerky Mix

Make unbelievably delicious jerky at a fraction of the cost of commercial brands. Just blend Spice 'n Slice, spice mix with water; stir and knead well into lean ground game meat. Then shape, press and dry in the oven or dehydrator at 160°F (71°C) for about 4 hours.

Variation
To make flank steak jerky, use 1/4 cup (60 mL) of water and 1/4-inch strips of meat. Marinate overnight and dry as above.

YIELD about 24 strips		
2 lbs	**extra lean ground game meat**	908 g
1/4 cup	**water**	60 mL
1	**package of Spice 'n Slice spice mix**	1

Helpful Hints for Making Jerky

Follow the easy instructions on the box.

Use the leanest ground meat available at least 90% lean.

Keep the meat chilled for easier handling.

Use an oven, dehydrator or smoker to dry your jerky.

Yields approximately 50%, depending on meat and drying time.

Refrigerate or freeze finished product.

Goose Jerky

I clean the geese by removing the breast, thigh and leg meat. This makes the meat lean and leaves the fat and the mess with the skin. The following directions call for two packages of Spice 'n Slice Jerky Mix.

Grind up the deboned goose meat. This is so much easier than trying to cut even strips of meat, especially when using the leg meat and there are no scraps to throw away.

Break up any lumps in the jerky seasoning mix and combine the two packages before adding to the ground meat. Stir the meat and jerky mix together by hand or mixer until well blended. I sometimes add a little extra garlic powder, or pepper to taste.

Lay down two yardsticks or rulers. Place a piece of plastic bag or waxed paper on the sticks. Place a 1 tsp (5 mL) size drop of mixture on the plastic and lay another sheet on top.

With a rolling pin, roll the meat mixture out between the plastic and lay another sheet on top.

Simply dry in a dehydrator or in your home oven. If in your own it takes about 5 hours at 140°F (60°C). Perfect jerky every time. Store in your refrigerator or freezer. Although the jerky is dry and does not need refrigeration, it is stiff subject to molding on the outside if kept at room temperature for too long.

Homemade Pastrami

Make great homemade pastrami using corned meat (see recipe for curing, page 72) then cook it in a smoker with dry heat.

Method

Remove meat from the brine; rub liberally on all sides with a mixture of coarse black pepper, coriander and paprika. Place in smoker or oven at 130°F (54°C). Hold this temperature for about 1 hour or until the surface of the meat is dry. Increase temperature gradually to 200–220°F (93–104°C) and hold until an internal temperature of 175–180°F (79–82°C) is obtained. Remove from oven or smoker and allow to cool for several hours before chilling overnight in refrigerator.

To serve, slice thinly and place into a cooking pan with several cups of water and cook 15–20 minutes until steamed and heated throughout.

Serve in a sandwich on rye bread with some mustard of your choice.

Note: The curing process is critical in the manufacture of smoked and cooked meat to prevent food poisoning.

Pepperoni

This is everybody's favorite for a spicy taste and it's easy. Combine one packet of pepperoni mix with water and add ground meat. Roll into logs and bake for one hour at 300°F (150°C). No casings are needed. Great for pizza, lunches, snacks, casseroles and flavoring spaghetti sauce.

Bulk Sausage Recipes 10-Pound Batches

Fresh Polish Sausage

YIELD about 10 lbs		
8 lbs	**venison trimmings**	3.6 kg
2 lbs	**beef fat**	908 g
4 tbsp	**salt**	60 mL
2 cups	**ice water**	500 mL
1 tbsp	**coarse black pepper**	15 mL
2 tsp	**marjoram**	10 mL
2	**cloves of fresh garlic**	2
2 tbsp	**granulated sugar**	30 mL

It is best to keep all ingredients, spices and meat, in the refrigerator overnight to keep it good and cold. Cut the meat and fat into workable size pieces to put through your grinder. Grind meat and fat together using 1/4-inch or 3/8-inch plate. Add and mix in all the spices and ice water thoroughly. Be sure that the meat is kept cold. Remove all clots, chords, etc. Do not let sausage warm up any more than necessary during processing. Stuff into hog casings about 35–38 mm. Make them about 16 inches long leaving 2 to 3 inches of casing on each end. Tie the two ends together to form a ring. After all meat is stuffed into casings and tied, hang in refrigerator several hours. Package and freeze as soon as possible. To cook sausages, place in saucepan of cold water and slowly bring to a boil.

Summer Sausage Bologna

Mix package contents with water and blend thoroughly with ground meat. Divide into 2 portions and shape into compact rolls approximately 12 inches long. No casings are needed. Place the rolls onto a wire rack with a drip pan and bake one hour at 300°F (150°C). This is a delicious mild-tasting sausage.

YIELD about 2 lbs

1	**package of**	1
	Summer Sausage Bologna Mix	
1/3 cup	**water**	75 mL
2 lbs	**ground meat**	908 g

Southern Style Sausage – Spicier than Country Style Sausage

A spicier homemade sausage mix that makes that perfect complement to any meal. At breakfast, on pizzas, casseroles, spaghetti or in your own favorite recipe. Bake broil, or fry. Great as a poultry marinade for the broiler or grill.

YIELD about 2 lbs

1	**package of**	1
	Southern Style Sausage Mix	
2 lbs	**ground meat**	908 g

Country Style Sausage

Now you can enjoy the great maple taste of country style sausages prepared fresh in your own kitchen. Use the "Country Spiced" blend to create plump, juicy sausages from ground meat that are ready to eat in minutes. Perfect for breakfast or anytime. (Prepare same as Southern Style Sausage). Great as a poultry marinade for the broiler or grill.

YIELD about 2 lbs

1	**package of**	1
	Country Spiced Sausage Mix	
2 lbs	**ground meat**	908 g

Smoked Breakfast Sausage

YIELD about 10 lbs

8 lbs	**venison trimmings**	3.6 kg
2 lbs	**beef fat**	908 g
6 tbsp	**salt**	90 mL
2 cups	**ice water**	500 mL
1 tsp	**ground white pepper**	5 mL
2 tbsp	**powdered dextrose**	30 mL
1 tsp	**ground ginger**	5 mL
1 tbsp	**ground nutmeg**	15 mL
1 tbsp	**sage**	15 mL
2 tsp (level)	**powder cure**	10 mL
2 cups	**soy protein powder**	500 mL

You may purchase the necessary, but hard to find ingredients for this sausage recipe directly from (Riverside Retreat in Newport PA). They have the correct amount of cure and dextrose and soy protein powder for a 10-pound batch of this sausage. You add the meat, fat and spices.

Again it is best to keep all ingredients, spices and meat in the refrigerator overnight to keep it good and cold. Pre-mix the dry spices to ensure even distribution of the cure. Cut the meat and fat into workable size pieces to put through your grinder. Grind meat and fat together using a 3/16 inch plate. Add and mix in all the spices and ice water thoroughly. Be sure that the meat is kept cold. Remove all blood clots, chords, etc. Stuff into lamb casings of about 24–26 mm or small hog casings will work as well. Form into 4-inch links by twisting the casings as you stuff the sausage, twist in opposite directions as you fill the case. (This gets easier after you do it a few times). If several pieces of casing are needed, tie the ends together to make into one long sausage. Do not let sausage warm up any more than necessary during processing.

Salami

YIELD about 2 lbs

2 lbs	**ground meat**	908 g
1	**package of Salami Mix**	1
1/3 cup	**water**	75 mL

Simply mix one packet of premium spice blend with water; stir in ground meat of your choice. Shape into logs and bake one hour. No casings are needed. Add garlic for a spicier flavor.

Penny Log Roll

Use your choice of Salami, Summer Sausage, Pepperoni or Jerky Mix with ground meat. For best results, refrigerate for an hour or more to allow the meat mixture to become firm for easier handling. On a piece of plastic wrap, shape the meat into a rectangle about 10- x 12-inches.

Spread desired filling (cream cheese or Velveeta-type cheese) over the meat leaving a 1-inch border. Starting at the long edge, roll the meat into a firm log sealing seam and both ends securely. You may want to wrap it back in the plastic wrap and refrigerate for awhile longer.

Place on a wire rack over a drip pan and bake as directed, 300°F (150°C) for 1 hour. Allow the log to cool thoroughly before slicing. Refrigerate or freeze.

YIELD about 2 lbs		
2 lbs	**ground hamburger** of your choice	908 g
1	**package of Salami, Summer Sausage, Pepperoni or Jerky**	1
	cream cheese or Velveeta cheese for spreading	

Fresh Breakfast Sausage

It is best to keep all ingredients, spices and meat, in the refrigerator overnight to keep it good and cold. Cut the meat and fat into workable size pieces to put through your grinder. Grind meat and fat together using a 3/16 inch plate. Add and mix in all the spices and ice water thoroughly. This may be used as is or stuffed into hog castings of about 28–30 mm or 22–24 mm lamb casings. Be sure that the meat is kept cold. Remove all blood clots, chords, etc. Do not let sausage warm up any more than necessary during processing. Package and freeze as soon as possible.

YIELD 10 lbs		
8 lbs	**venison trimmings**	3.6 kg
2 lbs	**beef fat**	908 g
4 tbsp	**salt**	60 mL
2 cups	**ice water**	500 mL
1 tbsp	**ground white pepper**	15 mL
2 tbsp	**rubbed sage**	30 mL
1 tbsp	**thyme**	15 mL
1 tsp	**ground hot red pepper** optional	5 mL
1 tbsp	**granulated sugar**	15 mL

Fresh Italian Sausage

YIELD 10 lbs

8 lbs	**venison trimmings**	3.6 kg
2 lbs	**beef fat**	908 g
5 tbsp	**salt**	75 mL
2 cups	**ice water**	500 mL
1 tbsp	**cracked black pepper**	15 mL
1 tbsp	**granulated sugar**	15 mL
3 tbsp	**crushed hot pepper**	45 mL
1 tsp	**caraway seeds**	5 mL
1 tbsp	**coriander**	15 mL

It is best to keep all ingredients, spices and meat, in the refrigerator overnight to keep good and cold. Cut the meat and fat into workable size pieces to put through your grinder. Grind meat and fat together using a 1/2-inch or 3/8-inch plate. Add and mix in all the spices and ice water thoroughly. This may be used as is or stuffed into hog casings of about 32–35 mm casings. Be sure that the meat is kept cold. Remove all blood clots, chords, etc. Do not let sausage warm up anymore than necessary during processing. Package and freeze as soon as possible.

Preparation of Salami, Summer, Bologna and Pepperoni

Use ground chuck quality ground hamburger or if you're using lean game meat, add some suet. or use ground beef and/or pork for a portion of your total ground meat (i.e. 1/3 pork with 2/3 game meat or 1/4 pork, 1/4 beef with 1/2 game meat).

Don't overcook. Bake just one hour. Finished product has a reddish color.

Those on low sodium diets can eliminate all or a portion of the cure package (small packet).

Preparation of Country Style Sausage and Southern Style Sausage

Following the first three hints under Salami, Summer Sausage, Bologna and Pepperoni.

If you need to reduce the salt in your diet, either add less of the packet of spices to your 2 pounds of meat or increase the amount of meat per packet of spices.

The Beach Bungalow Beto's Jerked Gator

Blend all ingredients, varying the heat as desired. Use the water to vary the thickness for clinging on spareribs or slopping up on the plate. Rub it on and refrigerate overnight. Tomorrow invite some friends.

YIELD about 2 1/2 cups

1 cup	allspice	250 mL
3	scotch bonnets or habeneros seeded and chopped	3
1-2	chipotle (smoked) pepper diced	1-2
10	scallions chopped	10
1/2 cup	onion chopped	125 mL
4	cloves garlic chopped	4
4	bay leaves crushed	4
1	3-inch piece ginger peeled and chopped	1
1/3 cup	thyme	75 mL
1 tsp	fresh ground nutmeg	5 mL
1 tsp	ground cinnamon	5 mL
1 tsp	salt	5 mL
1 tbsp	ground black pepper	15 mL
1/4 cup	olive oil	60 mL
1/4 cup	lime juice	60 mL
	water	

Award Winning Marinade For Game

Combine all ingredients in small container with lid. Cover and shake mixing well. Marinate game for two hours or overnight.

YIELD 2 cups

3/4 cup	Port	175 mL
1-1/4 cups	olive oil	310 mL
3	springs of tarragon	3
2	parsley stalks	2
1	large celery stalk coarsely chopped	1
1	small onion thinly sliced	1
6	peppercorns	6
1/8 tsp	sage	0.5 mL
1 tsp	lemon peel slivered	5 mL

Small Game with Honey-Mustard Sauce

YIELD 3/4 cup

1/2 cup	**honey**	125 mL
1/4 cup	**yellow mustard**	60 mL
2 tbsp	**lemon juice**	30 mL
1 tsp	**salt**	5 mL

This easy to make sauce is a wonderful accompaniment for rabbit, squirrel, quail or pheasant cooked on the grill.

Mix all ingredients and use to baste game during last 10 minutes of cooking time. Heat the remaining sauce and ladle over meat hot off the grill.

Paprika-Pepper Breakfast Venison Medallion Rub and Oil

1 tsp	**paprika**	5 mL
1/2 tsp	**onion powder**	2 mL
1/2 tsp	**garlic salt**	2 mL
1/2 tsp	**black pepper** fresh ground	2 mL
1/4 tsp	**white pepper**	1 mL
	dash of cayenne pepper	

SKILLET OIL

1 tbsp	**extra virgin olive oil**	15 mL
1 tbsp	**butter or margarine**	15 mL

Make a rub by thoroughly combining all spices in a small bowl. Pierce each piece of meat all over on both sides with a fork. Sprinkle each side with rub mixture (lightly if you prefer a less spicy taste, heavily for real pizzazz), and press it into the meat. Heat olive oil and butter or margarine over medium heat in a small black-iron skillet. Stir to mix. Sear each side of the venison pieces in the hot oil/butter mixture.

French Mustard

YIELD 3/4 cup

1/2 cup	**dry mustard**	125 mL
1/4 cup	**beer**	60 mL
1/2 tsp	**salt**	2 mL
3 tsp	**wine vinegar**	15 mL

Combine all ingredients in a small bowl and mix well. Serve with wild game sausages.

Hunter's Mustard

Stick onion with cloves. In a medium-size bowl, combine onion, garlic and vinegar; cover and refrigerate for 2 to 3 hours. Pour off liquid and reserve. Discard onion and garlic. In a medium-size bowl, slowly stir 1/2 cup (125 mL) reserved vinegar into the dry mustard. In an enamel or stainless steel saucepan boil remaining vinegar and bay leaf, covered, about three minutes. Add honey, basil, marjoram, turmeric, tarragon, horseradish, cayenne, and white pepper to the mustard mixture. Return to pan and bring to a boil; cook, stirring constantly, 6 minutes. Pour into hot, scaled half-pint jar, leaving 1/4-inch headspace. Seal and process in a boiling water bath for 15 minutes. If you're not going to process, cool mustard before pouring into jar. Refrigerate after opening.

YIELD 1 1/4 cups		
1	**medium onion** peeled	1
4	**whole cloves**	4
2	**garlic cloves** thinly sliced	2
1-1/4 cups	**cider vinegar**	310 mL
1	**bay leaf**	1
1 cup	**dry mustard**	250 mL
1 tsp	**honey**	5 mL
1/4 tsp	**basil** dried	1 mL
1/4 tsp	**ground marjoram**	1 mL
1/4 tsp	**turmeric**	1 mL
1/8 tsp	**tarragon**	0.5 mL
	cayenne pepper and white pepper to taste	
1 tsp	**homemade horseradish** (optional) creamy	5 mL

Marinade for Venison Kabob's

Mix marinade ingredients thoroughly in a zip-seal freezer bag. Add meat and marinate overnight in the refrigerator. Pour off marinade. Skewer meat, vegetables and fruit and grill to desired doneness.

YIELD 1 1/3 cups		
1/2 cup	**red wine vinegar**	125 mL
1/2 cup	**vegetable oil**	125 mL
1/3 cup	**onion** chopped	75 mL
1 tbsp	**Worcestershire sauce**	15 mL
1	**garlic clove** minced, or 1/2 tsp (2 mL) garlic powder	1
1 tbsp	**unseasoned meat tenderizer**	15 mL
1/4 tsp	**black pepper**	1 mL

Quail Plum Sauce

Thoroughly mix all condiments and spices. Brush quail with plum sauce and bake. Roast quail uncovered at 375°F (190°C) in a glass baking dish for 30 minutes. Serve with the remaining plum sauce heated and presented in a gravy boat. The sauce would be enough for six quail.

YIELD 1 1/2 cups

1 cup	**plum jelly**	250 mL
2 tbsp	**ketchup**	30 mL
2 tbsp	**apple cider vinegar**	30 mL
1/2 tsp	**dry mustard**	2 mL
4 tbsp	**soy sauce**	60 mL

Wild Game Burgundy Mustard

Chop the pickles and tarragon very fine and blend with the mustard. Garnish with finely chopped pickle. Use this mustard with thin slices of cold venison on thin sliced dark bread or on French bread.

YIELD 2 1/4 cups

2 cups	**Dijon mustard**	500 mL
12	**small sour pickles** chopped	12
1	**small sweet pickle** chopped	1
1 tsp	**dried tarragon** or 1-1/2 tbsp. (7 mL) fresh tarragon	5 mL

Sutton's Special Venison Marinade

Mix all ingredients, and pour over deer steak or loin in a zip-seal freezer bag. Seal the bag and refrigerate 1 to 4 hours, or overnight. Remove meat from marinade, and cook to desired degree of doneness on the grill or beneath the broiler.

YIELD 1 cup

1	**garlic clove** sliced and mashed	1
1 tbsp	**brown sugar**	15 mL
1/2 tsp	**each lemon pepper spice, ground ginger, fresh ground pepper**	7 mL
1 tbsp	**peanut or vegetable oil**	15 mL
2 tbsp	**water**	30 mL
1/4 cup	**soy sauce**	60 mL

Elegant Bird Marinade

Combine ingredients and heat in heavy saucepan and simmer for 15 minutes. Marinate game birds for two hours before roasting. Use for small or large game.

YIELD 1 1/2 cups

1-1/3 cups	**dry red wine**	325 mL
1/4 cup	**oil**	60 mL
12	**juniper berries** crushed	12
3	**bay leaves**	3
2	**garlic cloves** crushed	2

Curry and Honey Duck Glaze

Rub the ducks inside and out with curry powder mixed with garlic, turmeric, and Tabasco sauce. Roast over medium coals. During last half-hour of grilling time, baste frequently with honey mixture.

YIELD 1 cup

RUB

2 tbsp	**curry powder**	30 mL
2	**cloves of garlic** finely chopped	2
1 tsp	**turmeric**	5 mL
1/2 tsp	**Tabasco sauce**	2 mL

HONEY MIXTURE

1/2 cup	**honey**	125 mL
1/4 cup	**orange juice**	60 mL
1/4 cup	**lemon juice**	60 mL

Cranberry-Orange Sauce

Combine the cranberries, sugar, orange juice, salt and Port in a large saucepan. Bring to a slow boil then cover. Reduce heat and simmer. Serve warm or cold with game.

YIELD 4 1/2 cups

1 lb	**cranberries** fresh frozen	454 g
2 cups	**sugar**	500 mL
1/2 cup	**orange juice**	125 mL
1/8 tsp	**salt**	0.5 mL
1/4 cup	**Port**	60 mL

Savory Game Bird Cream

YIELD 1/2 cup		
6 tbsp	**cream cheese** softened	90 mL
	whipping cream	
2-1/2 oz.	**can Paté de Foie Gras** purchased in specialty stores	82.5 g
1 tbsp	**Madeira**	15 mL

Beat cream cheese on high speed to a light consistency. Add enough whipping cream to moisten. Break up the paté with a fork and add the Madeira gradually, blending well. Combine the cream cheese mixture and the paté thoroughly. Place in bowl and serve with game birds.

Quail Marinade

YIELD 3/4 cup		
1/2 cup	**vegetable oil**	125 mL
3 tbsp	**lemon juice**	45 mL
	salt and pepper to taste	
1-1/2 tsp	**onion** grated	7 mL
	pinch of nutmeg or ginger	

Combine ingredients and mix well. Marinate quail for one hour before cooking.

Whiskey Game Marinade

YIELD 1/2 cup		
1 tbsp	**black pepper**	15 mL
2 tbsp	**olive oil**	30 mL
2 tbsp	**wine vinegar**	30 mL
	salt to taste	
1/2 tsp	**sugar**	2 mL
3 tbsp	**whiskey**	45 mL

Combine olive oil, black pepper, wine vinegar and salt. Marinate game meat at room temperature for three hours. Grill meat, sprinkle with sugar and warmed whiskey.

Goose Glaze

YIELD 2 1/4 cups		
1 cup	**pineapple juice**	250 mL
1 cup	**Marsala wine**	250 mL
1/4 cup	**orange-flavoured liqueur**	60 mL
1	**zest of one orange**	1
1	**orange** peeled and chopped	1

Combine all of the ingredients in heavy skillet; heat on low until slightly thickened. Pour over goose and continue to cook goose in the oven until desired doneness.

English Pub Mustard for Game

Combine all ingredients except ale or beer. Then add beer slowly. Blend until smooth and creamy. Refrigerate.

YIELD 2 1/2 cups		
1 cup	**dry mustard**	250 mL
1/2 cup	**brown sugar**	125 mL
1 tsp	**salt**	5 mL
1/4 tsp	**turmeric**	1 mL
1 cup	**ale or flat beer**	250 mL

Chef Angelo's Game Sauce

Lightly brown carrot and onion with butter. Stir in the flour and cook until flour turns golden brown. Add chicken or beef bouillon and tomato purée. Mix well with wire whip and cook over low heat until smooth. Add bay leaf, thyme, parsley Simmer for additional 15 minutes.

In another pan put vinegar, leftover marinade, crushed peppercorns and red wine. Boil until liquid reduces to one-third of original quantity. Strain the sauce into the reduced vinegar mixture and cook for 10 minutes, skimming frequently. Strain and add 1/2 cup (125 mL) of your favorite red wine. Bring to boil and serve.

YIELD 6 cups		
1	**carrot** diced	1
1	**onion** diced	1
6 tbsp	**butter**	90 mL
1 cup	**flour**	250 mL
3 cups	**chicken or beef bouillon**	750 mL
1 cup	**tomato purée**	250mL
1	**bay leaf**	1
	pinch of thyme	
	few springs of parsley	
1/2 cup	**vinegar**	125 mL
1/2 cup	**leftover marinade**	125 mL
4	**crushed peppercorns**	4
1/2 cup	**red wine**	125 mL

Quail Basting Sauce

Combine all ingredients. Simmer in saucepan for 10 minutes. Add salt and pepper to taste. Baste quail often.

YIELD 1 1/2 cups		
1 cup	**ketchup**	250 mL
2 tbsp	**brown sugar**	30 mL
2 tbsp	**cider vinegar**	30 mL
1 tbsp	**Worcestershire sauce**	15 mL
1 tsp	**prepared mustard**	5 mL
1/4 tsp	**garlic salt**	1 mL
2 tbsp	**onion** grated	30 mL
1	**small garlic clove** minced	1

Herb and Buttermilk Game Bird Marinade

3/4 cup	**buttermilk**	175 mL
2 tbsp	**Dijon mustard**	30 mL
2	**garlic cloves** minced	2
2 tsp	**dried oregano**	10 mL
2 tsp	**dried basil**	10 mL
2 tsp	**ground thyme**	10 mL
2 tsp	**rosemary leaves**	10 mL
1/4 tsp	**salt**	1 mL
1/4 tsp	**fresh black pepper**	1 mL

Combine all the ingredients in order and set aside. Clean and cut birds. Marinade in the refrigerator for 3 hours or overnight. Barbecue or cook birds in the oven. The birds can also be sautéed in a hot skillet and finished in the oven at 350°F (175°C) until cooked to desired doneness.

Spice Blend for Charred Venison

1 tsp	**whole cumin** toasted, ground	5 mL
1 tsp	**whole mustard seed** toasted, ground	5 mL
1/2 tsp	**whole allspice** ground	2 mL
1/2 tsp	**whole cloves** ground	2 mL
1 tsp	**garlic powder**	5 mL
1 tsp	**chili powder**	5mL
2 tsp	**sea salt**	10 mL
1 tsp	**ground black pepper**	1tsp

Combine mustard seed and cumin seed in a sauté pan and place over medium heat for about 2 minutes, shaking often. You should begin to smell a toasty aroma. Set aside to cool. Grind in a spice mill. Combine all ingredients together well. Keep in an airtight container.

Roast Duck Honey Glaze

1 cup	**apricot, cherry** **or peach preserves**	250 mL
1/2 cup	**clover honey**	125 mL
1 tbsp	**Brandy**	15 mL
1 tbsp	**Grand Marnier** **or other orange-flavoured liqueur**	15 mL

Combine all ingredients in small saucepan on medium heat, blend well. Coat duck or goose with this glaze the last 15 minutes of roasting; return to oven until glaze caramelizes.

Credits

It isn't with out help, encouragement, special organizations, and friends that one is able to even begin the publication of a book. I want to recognize all of those very special people.

Photo Credits

Sheina Wait
Moose Jaw, Saskatchewan

Four Winds, Prairie
Photography
Wayne Shiels
Warman, Saskatchewan

New West Foods
1120 Lincoln Street, Suite 905
Denver, Co
Cover, insert pages

Credits

Seattle's Finest Exotic Meats
17532 Aurora Avenue
Seattle Washington

Nick's Riverside Retreat
Newport, PA

Hill Foods Ltd
#109 – 3650 Bonneville Place
Burnaby, British Columbia
Canada V3N 4T7

Arkansas Game and
Fish Commission
2 Natural Resources Drive
Little Rock, Arkansas 72205

Chef Les Kincaid
Las Vegas, Nevada

Chef Tim Schafer
Morristown, New Jersey

Richard Kutas
America's Formost
Sausage Maker

The Red Castle Inn
Nevada City, California

Cliff House at Pikes Peak
Manitou Springs, Colorado
Chef Craig Hartman

Millbrook Inn & Restaurant
Waitsfield, Vermont

Bluebonnet Venison Farms
San Antonio, Texas

Broken Arrow Ranch
Ingram, Texas

Three Chimneys Inn and
Restaurants
Durham, New Hampshire

L'Auberge Provencale
White Post, Virginia

The Bloom House
San Diego, California

Oceanwood Country Inn
Mayne Island,
British Columbia

The Inn at New Berlin
New Berlin, Pennsylvania

Hidden Creek Ranch
Harrison, Idaho

Cougar Ranch
Missoula, Montana

Alisal Guest Ranch
and Resort
Solvang, California

Casa Vieja Restaurant
Corrales, New Mexico

The River Plantation Inn
Dover, Tennessee

Borga's Hideaway
Scottsdale, Arizona

Inn on the Twenty
Jordan, Ontario

Newberry Beefalo Farm
Big rapids, Michigan

Kea Lani Hotel
Wailea, Maui

Roland's Place
New Haven, Vermont

The Farm House
Montrose, West Virginia

Grandma La Mure's
Spice'n Slice Mixes for
Ground Meats
215 West Lodge Drive
Tempe Arizona

Index

Index

Index